Finding God

Finding God

JOSEPH HAWARD
Foreword by Simon Hall

WIPF & STOCK · Eugene, Oregon

FINDING GOD

Copyright © 2025 Joseph Haward. All rights reserved. Except for brief quotations in critical publications or reviews, no part of this book may be reproduced in any manner without prior written permission from the publisher. Write: Permissions, Wipf and Stock Publishers, 199 W. 8th Ave., Suite 3, Eugene, OR 97401.

Wipf & Stock
An Imprint of Wipf and Stock Publishers
199 W. 8th Ave., Suite 3
Eugene, OR 97401

www.wipfandstock.com

PAPERBACK ISBN: 979-8-3852-3982-5
HARDCOVER ISBN: 979-8-3852-3983-2
EBOOK ISBN: 979-8-3852-3984-9

04/11/25

Scripture quotations marked (NRSV) are from the New Revised Standard Version Bible, copyright © 1989 National Council of the Churches of Christ in the United States of America. Used by permission. All rights reserved worldwide.

Scripture quotations marked (NKJV) are taken from the New King James Version®. Copyright © 1982 by Thomas Nelson. Used by permission. All rights reserved.

For Sarah, Cas, Judy, Sarah, and Hannah.

You are loved. And you are not alone. That is God.
Erin Greene, *Midnight Mass*

Brooks sat and stared at the white breath as it escaped the praying men's mouths. If he were still a religious man he might have seen it like the smoke of an offering, floating towards the heavens, petitioning God with the smell of lives given in sacrifice.
Joe Haward, *Every Last Drop*

Ask, and it shall be given to you; seek, and you shall find; knock, and it shall be opened to you. For everyone who asks receives, and everyone who seeks finds, and to everyone who knocks it shall be opened.
Jesus, *Matt 7:7–8*

Contents

Foreword by Simon Hall		ix
Preface		xiii
Introduction		xxi
1	The Scapegoat	1
2	The Cry of Achan	7
3	Monuments of Murder	16
4	Acts 5:1–11	22
5	Genesis and Acts	38
6	Mercy Not Sacrifice	45
7	The Victim's Story	54
Conclusion		63
Appendix I: Judas Iscariot		71
Appendix II: Lucifer		82
Appendix III: Death of the Firstborn		86
Appendix IV: Holiness		91
Bibliography		95

Foreword

JOSEPH HAWARD IS A brave human being. You have in your hand an exercise, not in fearlessness, but in confronting our deepest fears head on and wrestling them into submission.

What are our deepest fears? Perhaps the deepest fear of all is that our lives have no value, purpose, or meaning. Or that we are alone and unloved. In religious language, we fear that behind our rituals lies a perverse and unreliable deity that dabbles in our lives for reasons we can never fathom. For those of us that own the name of Christ, this deity haunts our dreams, heckling from the wings that the revelation of God in Jesus of Nazareth is a phantom; the vengeful and bloodthirsty god that ruled throughout history has killed Jesus and taken the reins once more. Can we find a god worthy of the name? Joe knows that if that god is to be found in the Christian tradition, we must take the Bible seriously. But not in the way you might expect.

Most of us cower from biblical texts that claim to reveal the divine mind, only to show us a god who resembles nothing so much as the puppet character Mr. Punch: grotesque, volatile, and prone to rain down disproportionate violence upon his nearest and dearest, laughing as he does so. As Paul Simon might say, Joe doesn't find this stuff amusing any more. Joe believes that the *abba* of Jesus of Nazareth is nothing like Mr. Punch, something that the whole world can receive as good news! Joe has a toolkit that enables him to dismantle not just Mr. Punch but the entire puppet show.

Foreword

The toolkit Joe uses comes from a master craftsman: the late anthropologist and cultural commentator René Girard. Girard offers all of us a way to see our human condition with perhaps as much clarity as is possible in this life. As the apostle Paul wrote, "For now we only see a reflection, as in a mirror, but then we will see face to face" (1 Cor 13:12 NRSV). Life often feels as though we are on the reflective side of a one-way mirror: our inquiries into what lies beyond result in a partial self-knowledge, but the darkness beyond remains a mystery. Girard offers us the best kind of self-knowledge, the kind that invites a complete reconfiguring of the way we see ourselves and our relationships with each other. This reconfiguration inevitably results in a change in the way that we see God, who remains behind the two-way mirror, but is nonetheless revealed in new ways as we see each other "face to face."

Unlike the early modern biblical scholars, among whom Rudolf Bultmann was the most (in)famous, Girard was not interested in "demythologizing" the biblical text, as if the only truth to be found was in some plain idea of "historical fact" (such a thing is a myth of a different kind). Rather, Girard was fascinated by the very process of mythologization, of how humans make sense of important events—particularly violence. Perhaps this mythologization happened because events seemed random, meaningless, or cruel. Perhaps the plain and obvious meaning was too terrifying to admit. Whatever the reason, Girard saw a repeating pattern of mythologization happening throughout literature, culture, and history.

When it comes to reading the Jewish and Christian Scriptures, I suspect many of us believe that at least some part of the story is steeped in a form of mythological reinterpretation. (If you are the kind of person who believes that the creation narratives of Gen 1–3 are either 100 percent scientifically and historically accurate or they are nothing, this is probably not the book for you.) I suspect most of us see the very earliest stories found in Gen 1–11 as having primarily mythological purposes. I imagine we see history emerging out of this foundation, such that by the time of the Davidic kingdom, or certainly by the time the Jews returned from exile, we are dealing with historic events that have some degree of theological interpretation. The first story that Joe addresses in this book sits within this hinterland, in which mythology and history dance awkwardly. The awkwardness comes from the uncertainty as to who is leading whom, and we bring our own prior commitments to bear when adjudicating the ensuing conflict. If we are looking for a way out—for ourselves and God—of the sudden and brutal intracommunity violence that results in the death of Achan and his whole household, Joe is able to bring Girard to our aid. This is an old, old story from a time before history, and giving it a new spin feels reasonable and saves us from confronting the Stone Age god depicted in the text.

But this is where Joe's bravery comes to the fore: he explores two examples from the central stories of Jesus and the founding of the church. Joe does this because, like Girard, he believes that the mythologization of human violence continues to this day, so it is inevitable that it will crop up in the New Testament as well as the Old. Thus, the Christian Scriptures function as revelation in multiple ways: they display how *mimesis* and *scapegoating* (terms that Joe explains in this book) create and perpetuate human violence *and* religion, demonstrating the apocalyptic ("unveiling") ministry and death of Jesus, and thus revealing the true nature of God.

If you have not read Girard, I expect reading this book will feel like wearing someone else's glasses. I have read some Girard, and am familiar with the works of others who toil to popularize his ideas, yet I found in this book several moments of disorientation, expecting at any moment to lose my footing. Yet the moments passed, and I learned to see familiar events in a new and revealing light. You are entitled to ask yourself, as I do, whether a twentieth century anthropologist really found the key to the Scriptures. It sounds like the plot of a Dan Brown novel. All I can do is call you back to the image of that mirror—that in seeing ourselves more clearly, we might see something of the one behind the mirror.

The stakes could not be higher. If God is like Mr. Punch, then Christians are right to promote vengeful and violent men into the leadership of our churches, institutions, and governments, because such people are indeed godlike. However, if God is like the *abba* of Jesus—if God is like Jesus himself, the forgiving victim—then the path we must take is very different.

The gospel of John contains these immortal lines: "No one has ever seen God. It is the only Son, himself God, who is close to the Father's heart, who has made him known" (John 1:18 NRSV). As I write these lines, I anticipate hearing them at a carol service in a couple of days. Even if Girard's glasses don't sit completely comfortably on your nose, I urge you to look for God in the same place as Joseph Haward: the person of Jesus. If God is like Jesus, the rest flows from that.

Simon Hall
Advent 2024

Preface

In 2012, when my eldest daughter was five years old, we were reading her children's Bible together before bedtime. We had been working through various stories from the Hebrew Scriptures, going back and forth according to what she was interested in at the time, and arrived at Exodus and the killing of the firstborn in Egypt. After reading about the death of the Egyptian children, my daughter paused, looked at me, and asked a question.

"Daddy," she began. "Why did God kill all those children?"

Although the killing of the firstborn was something I had reflected on many times, grappling with the ethical and theological questions it raised, there was something about the way my daughter asked the question that left me inwardly scrambling.

"Well," I stammered. "What do you think?"

She looked back at her Bible, examining the picture of an Egyptian father cradling the body of his dead child. "I don't know. It just doesn't sound like something Jesus would do."

This comment from my daughter threw me into a theological spin, one that I spent the next few years trying to pull out from.

I knew the standard responses to my daughter's question, and, as a church leader, had preached and taught about the holiness of God, the gravity of sin, the sacrifice of the Son, etc. Yet, prior to this bedtime theological examination, I had become increasingly unsure that the answers I had so often vehemently defended were satisfactory. Indeed, I had begun to wonder if they were answers at all. My daughter's question felt more like a confirmation that I needed to do a lot more work, and a lot more reading.

Preface

I read Calvin, Luther, the church mothers and fathers, Bonhoeffer, Ilia Delio, Julian of Norwich, Lossky, Rowan Williams, Michael Hardin, Joseph Ratzinger, Phyllis Trible, Stanley Hauerwas, Dr. Martin Luther King Jr., James Cone, David Bentley Hart, and Ilaria Ramelli. I read obscure theologians and philosophers, atheists, psychoanalysts, and anthropologists. I became obsessive for knowledge and understanding, searching for ways to help my daughter's question make sense to me: "Daddy, why did God kill all those children?"

This book is an attempt, in some way, at answering that question.

If there was one book that I read which changed my life completely, in a way that few others have, it was *Things Hidden Since the Foundation of the World* by René Girard. There is nothing new under the sun, but, after I had read that book, I felt as though I had woken up out of a long slumber. *Finding God* draws much from the influence of that book, as well as from many of my theological heroes, some of whom I named above.

Impulsive Gods

There is a long history within the church in seeking to understand divine violence. My daughter's question has been asked, in one form or another, by some of the finest theologians the church has ever produced. For instance, in the third century, Origen of Alexandria (ca. 185–ca. 253) maintained that the violence commanded by God in the Hebrew Scriptures was allegorical, and only a spiritual reading was possible or legitimate in these instances. Likewise, in the fourth century, Gregory of Nyssa (ca. 335–ca. 394), probably the greatest theologian in church history, produced the most remarkable allegorical reading of the book of Exodus called *The Life of Moses*. And Isaac of Nineveh (ca. 613–ca. 700), as we shall explore below, believed biblical literalists were, to put it mildly, out of their mind.

If these incredible thinkers and theologians could see a problem, then it would be arrogance on our part to dismiss such a problem out of hand. It might initially feel neat and tidy to tie off divine violence as an expression of God's hatred of sin—or dismiss it as a moral irrelevance because God can do "whatever God wants to do" as the ultimate giver and taker of life—but this will not do. Indeed, as we shall see, such answers become woefully inadequate the more you delve into the problem.

Divine justice cannot be an arbitrary judgment according to the whims and moods of the ultimate being. Indeed, the idea of God somehow being "caught off guard" by human action, and then responding to that action in wrath or despair, is theologically incoherent. If we were discussing the actions of the Greek gods, for instance, then it would not be unusual to find one of them acting impulsively, or in a fit of rage. Take Zeus, for example, a god prone to fits of rage, excessive lust, and the desire for power. When Prometheus tricks him, Zeus responds with a kind of impetuous anger reserved for toddlers or the emotionally stunted.

> Zeus who thunders on high was stung in spirit, and his dear heart was angered when he saw amongst men the far-seen ray of fire. Forthwith he made an evil thing for men as the price of fire.[1]

Today's depictions of the gods, such as Thor or Loki in the Marvel cinematic universe, follow in the footsteps of similar divine impulsivity and strong desire. These gods, whether Greek, Roman, Nordic, or countless other mythological beings from cultures through time and space, share in these very human traits, actions and reactions, integral to their character and power. These gods can very much be caught off guard, for they, no matter how powerful they might be, are not God in the fullest sense.

To speak of such gods is to recognize how, despite their power, each belongs, in some way, to *created* reality. Their existence is birthed from within the cosmos, in a myriad of supremely powerful circumstances. But that does not make them supreme in the ultimate sense.

---

1. Hesiod, *Theogony*, 560.

Preface

> Any gods who might be out there do not transcend nature but belong to it. . . . They exist in space and time, each of them is a distinct being rather than "being itself," and it is they who are dependent upon the universe for their existence rather than the reverse.[2]

Beliefs about fairies and gods, Hart continues, share the same conceptual space as our beliefs regarding gravity, photons, and organic cells. In other words, such things (if they exist at all) exist within a contingent reality, their possibility the result of something utterly "other." And that *other* is God.

To speak of God is not to speak of something supreme. God is not a "being among beings" as Paul Tillich once highlighted, or "one of a kind," but, rather, is being itself. God is not an object *par excellence*, existing somewhere "out there," a being that is something like us, only infinitely more powerful. Such a being would indeed be impressive, but it would not be the God of classical theism. Rather, God is being itself, the fount and source of all existence, and therefore could never be "caught off guard."

The actions of humanity do not "surprise" God. Things don't happen that God could not perceive. God does not wake up one day to find the world has moved on, and they didn't see it coming. So, *if* God is violent, then that violence is somehow integral to who God is. If indeed God did kill all the firstborn in Egypt, then God is acting not in petulance or exasperation but as an expression of eternal divine character.

God is the source from which all reality is derived, not an object within reality. In many ways it is easier to say that God *does not* exist, rather than trying to describe the way that God is present within reality. This is why the apophatic[3] tradition determined that it is easier to speak of what God *is not* rather than what God is.

> We cannot speak of God in his own nature directly, but only at best analogously, and even then, only in such a

---

2. Hart, *Experience of God*, 31.
3. Knowledge from negation.

way that the conceptual content of our analogies consists largely in our knowledge of all the things that God is not.[4]

Or, as Augustine (354–430) once put it, "*Si comprehendis, non est deus.*"[5]

If you comprehend it, it is not God.

God is beyond all definitions, yet, paradoxically, according to Christian tradition, defined in and through the person of Jesus. Who is God? "I am that I am." Unnameable. Gregory the Theologian (ca. 329–ca. 391), in one of the most majestic prayers ever recorded, puts it this way:

> O All Transcendent God, (and what other name could describe you?) what words can sing Your praises? No word does You justice. What mind can probe Your secrets? No mind can encompass You. You alone are beyond the power of speech, yet all that we speak stems from You. You alone are beyond the power of thought, yet all that we can conceive springs from You. All things proclaim You, those endowed with reason and those bereft of it. All the expectation and pain of the world coalesces in You. All things utter a prayer to You, a silent hymn composed by You. You sustain everything that exists, and all things move together at Your command. You are the goal of all that exists. You are one and you are all, yet You are none of the things that exist, neither a part nor the whole. You can avail Yourself of any name; how shall I call You, the only unnamable? All-transcendent God![6]

I could write an entire book on this prayer alone. The language beautifully encapsulates the very best of Cappadocian theology, namely, how God is the beginning and end of all things, the one who is "all in all,"[7] and in whom "all things" are held together.[8] Gregory of

---

4. Hart, *Experience of God*, 142.
5. Augustine, *Patrologia Latina*, 663.
6. Papavassiliou, *Ancient Faith Prayer Book*, 154.
7. 1 Cor 15:28. Unless otherwise indicated, all biblical quotations are taken from Hart, *New Testament*.
8. Col 1:17.

Preface

Nyssa believed all humanity looked with "yearning" towards their ultimate unification in Christ,[9] while his sister, Makrina, spoke poetically of every "economy" in the universe moving towards "the transcendent good of the universe," namely Christ himself.[10]

Gregory's prayer above brings these ideas together with majestic clarity: all things are being gathered together in God because every part of created reality is bound to its Creator, every desire—known and unknown—yearning ultimately for its telos (goal), and that goal is Christ.

Yet, as Gregory's prayer also highlights, how we speak of God is filled with difficulty. Indeed, how do we define the actions and character of this undefinable one within Scripture? For some, it comes easy enough. The prominent atheist, Richard Dawkins, says,

> The God of the Old Testament is arguably the most unpleasant character in all fiction: jealous and proud of it; a petty, unjust, unforgiving control-freak; a vindictive, bloodthirsty ethnic cleanser; a misogynistic, homophobic, racist, infanticidal, genocidal, filicidal, pestilential, megalomaniacal, sadomasochistic, capriciously malevolent bully.[11]

While it *might* be easy to dismiss this theological assessment by Dawkins as crude and naive, take note of a sermon preached by the Puritan Jonathan Edwards (1703–1758) on July 8, 1741, warning his congregation about the eternal state of human beings in hell.

> When God beholds the ineffable extremity of your case, and sees your torment to be so vastly disproportioned to your strength, and sees how your poor soul is crushed, and sinks down, as it were, into an infinite gloom; he will have no compassion upon you, he will not forbear the executions of his wrath, or in the least lighten his hand; there shall be no moderation or mercy, . . . he will have no regard to your welfare. . . . Nothing shall be withheld.

---

9. See Gregory of Nyssa, *Homilies on the Beatitudes*, 55–56.

10. Gregory of Nyssa, *On the Soul and Resurrection*, quoted in Pelikan, *Christianity and Classical Culture*, 325.

11. Dawkins, *God Delusion*, 31.

> . . . You will be wholly lost and thrown away of God, as to any regard to your welfare. God will have no other use to put you to, but to suffer misery; you shall be continued in being to no other end; for you will be a vessel of wrath fitted to destruction; and there will be no other use of this vessel, but to be filled full of wrath. God will be so far from pitying you when you cry to him, that it is said he will only "laugh and mock."[12]

This language might feel uncomfortable to our modern ears, which is, in part, why the message of the New Atheists, specifically about the "God of the Old Testament," resonates with so many. We want a God who is loving and compassionate, and anything other than that feels utterly abhorrent. But perhaps more than that, we want a God who *makes sense*. As human beings, we recognize love, kindness, compassion, and forgiveness when we experience it. So when God is apparently unable, or unwilling, to do the very things we are capable of, it makes little sense.[13]

In the main, Western churches do indeed preach about the love of God and God's compassion upon humanity. Yet there is a "dark side" to this God. Yes, God is love, many of these churches will say, but God is also holy.[14] These churches will insist that God *must* deal with sin, that in turn leads to *how* God deals with sin. Which returns us to my daughter's question—Why did God kill all those children?—and the question as to how we speak of this "Unnameable One" that we see in Scripture.

Is it possible to comprehend who this God is? Is it possible to stay faithful to Scripture and discover a God who is *not* violent? Did God really kill all those children?[15]

---

12. Edwards, "Sinners," para. 29.

13. A not insignificant point about some versions of the atonement is that it appears God is unwilling to do the very thing he commands us to do, namely, forgive enemies.

14. See appendix 4 for a word on holiness.

15. For a specific response to the killing of the firstborn in Egypt, see appendix 3.

Preface

These are the questions that shape the very heart of this book. You will be the judge as to how well such questions will be handled in the following pages.

Rev. Joseph Haward
Devon, UK
Advent 2024

Introduction

BEING HUMAN MEANS LIVING in a violent world. Such is the ubiquitous nature of media today, news of human violence is easy to find. Whether humans have become more or less violent through history is not the focus of this book,[1] but that we *are* violent is not difficult to conclude.

Human violence can be traced throughout history, with stories of our violence found in Greek plays, medieval documents, and on our social media feeds. Our violence, and how we respond to such violence, is an ethical and moral issue. During the times of the Civil Rights Movement, for instance, the struggle for racial equality by the black community and the response to the violence committed against the black community were handled in different ways. Dr. Martin Luther King Jr. advocated for nonviolent resistance to such oppression, whereas Malcolm X called for a violent revolution. Both men fought for total emancipation for their black brothers and sisters, yet were divided in how such freedom was to be won, and what the end result should look like.

Human violence is not easily solved. For some, however, it is not something that needs to be solved as such, simply appropriately managed. Over recent years, certainly here in the UK, but common across Western democracies, there has been a call for the death penalty to be restored to deal with certain types of violence.

---

1. See Oka et al., "Population Is the Main Driver." The authors argue that, when "scaling is accounted for, we find no difference in conflict investment or lethality between small-scale and state societies." In other words, they argue that humanity is no more and no less violent today than it has ever been.

Introduction

However, those arguing for capital punishment often politicize such ideological pursuits, using nationalist rhetoric, framed within the language of fighting against a declining empire. State violence, they insist, is vital for the protection and flourishing of society; the threat of violence deters violence, so the argument goes. The evidence suggests otherwise. US states without the death penalty consistently record a lower homicide rate than those states with the death penalty.[2] Once again, however, the ethical arguments for or against state violence is not the focus of this book. I draw your attention to such arguments merely to point out that *who* is delivering the violence will often influence the argument as to whether such violence is deemed justified or not.[3] The *who* and the *why* shape the entire ethical issue for many people, especially when exploring "divine" violence in the Bible. And it is this violence that will be the focus of this book, particularly the violence specifically commanded by God, to be executed by people on God's behalf, as a sign of judgment upon another group of people.

The violence ascribed to God, or commanded by God in the Bible, is, for many people, an ethical conundrum. Indeed, for some it reveals why Christianity is morally indefensible. Richard Dawkins, in *The God Delusion*, highlights this point with great force, saying,

> The Bible story of Joshua's destruction of Jericho, and the invasion of the Promised Land in general, is morally indistinguishable from Hitler's invasion of Poland, or Saddam Hussein's massacres of the Kurds and the Marsh Arabs. The Bible may be an arresting and poetic work of fiction, but it is not the sort of book you should give your children to form their morals.[4]

---

2. See Death Penalty Information Center, "Murder Rate."

3. I find it fascinating that 75 percent of white evangelical Christians in America support the death penalty, yet if the same people were asked if they supported state executions in Saudi Arabia, for instance, most would likely oppose it.

4. Dawkins, *God Delusion*, 280.

INTRODUCTION

Dawkins, like the rest of the so-called New Atheists, is unambiguous as to his disdain of the God of the Bible. For him, God is a tyrant unequaled in cruelty, capriciousness, and moral failings. The late Christopher Hitchens is equally scathing, believing that we "ought to be glad that none of the religious myths has any truth to it, or in it. The Bible may, indeed does, contain a warrant for trafficking in humans, for ethnic cleansing, for slavery, for brideprice, and for indiscriminate massacre."[5]

While the broader arguments of the New Atheists *may* be easy to dismiss,[6] there is a fundamental "itch" that these particular arguments—especially surrounding God's involvement with violence—leave upon the consciousness of any curious person. Do we simply accept that the God of the Bible is irredeemable, a monster who, real or not, deserves nothing but scorn? Or is the violence ascribed to God fully justifiable, the actions of a holy God against a sinful world? Or do we throw it all away as pure myth, stories that have little to nothing to offer us moderns? Perhaps it is all analogy, language used to share deeper spiritual truths rather than historical facts? Maybe it is historically accurate, a literal account of how events unfolded? Are there two sides to God? How do we read the Bible?

Karl Barth believed there was a way through these challenges:

> If the fire of His wrath scorches us, it is because it is the fire of His wrathful love, and not his wrathful hate. Man has always stood up to the hatred of the gods. But God is not one of these gods of hatred. Man cannot stand up to His wrath because it is the wrath of His love. The reason why His curse falls so hard upon us is that it is

---

5. Hitchens, *God Is Not Great*, 102.

6. While I think that Dawkins, Hitchens, and Sam Harris are often clunky in their language, and incredibly lazy in their philosophical and hermeneutical approach to theology and Scripture, I do believe they sometimes ask the right questions, especially around the ethical and moral challenges of certain biblical passages. However, there are better apologists for atheism, and far more robust attacks against Christianity than the works of these three. For an excellent counter to the arguments of the New Atheists, as well as an insight into stronger arguments from other atheistic perspectives, see Hart, *Atheist Delusions*.

> surrounded by the rainbow of His covenant. It is the dark side of the blessing with which He has blessed us and wills to bless us. Those whom He loves He chastens.[7]

There are times when God acts in wrath, Barth concludes, but it is the wrath of love. Barth, like many before and after him, recognize the challenge within the text but, they would say, those challenges can be theologically held together. But can it be held together?

It is not disingenuous to suggest that what we have in Scripture are seemingly paradoxical moments where the God of love, who calls for forgiveness and blessing for enemies, is also the God of wrath, bringing down fire from the heavens upon the heads of false prophets, and commanding the slaughter of women and children. Theologians and church leaders attempt to harmonize the God of the Bible, finding a way to hold together the tension between grace and violence that exists within the text. In many ways it is a pastoral concern, a tension many local church ministers will be dealing with as they pastor their congregations.

I imagine that most church leaders will highlight the fact that, at some point in their ministry, someone within their congregation will have approached them about these very issues, pointing to various passages in Scripture that are not simply an itch upon their consciousness but an all-out rash, leaving them in a state of anxiety about their faith, and what to believe. I personally remember a church member who was very upset asking me about Isa 45:7 (NRSV).

> I form the light, and create darkness: I make peace, and create evil: I the Lord do all these things.

I muddled together an answer, as thoroughly perplexed by these words as the person asking me. How can it be, I thought to myself, that God "creates" evil? It was as though Scripture was painting *two sides* to God, a God very much of light and darkness. At the time I settled for such an idea, soothing myself with the belief that God's love has to be balanced with holiness, because sin cannot be overlooked. It didn't give anything like an adequate

---

7. Barth, *Church Dogmatics* 3/2:170.

INTRODUCTION

answer to the passage, but simply helped me move past the issue and never return.[8]

Such passages are not unusual within Scripture as God's compassion is held together with wrath, mercy with judgment, forgiveness with violence: the stories of Noah, Moses and the Exodus, the prophets of Baal, and perhaps even Ananias and Sapphira.[9]

What will not satisfy are glib answers and sidesteps, trying to pretend such questions are no questions at all. "If God said it, or did it, then it's good, and that's all that matters," is not an intellectual, emotional, or reasonable response; people deserve much more from their pastors and teachers. Equally, dismissing such passages as ancient superstition that have no importance for our modern world is lazy and unhelpful. *Something* is happening in these passages, and it is important to discover what that something is. Ultimately, we are trying to find out *who God is*.

Limping Christians

Like Jacob wrestling with God in the dark, wrestling as we wait for the dawn of the kingdom to break forth, we enter the biblical text seeking for God to bless us, refusing to let go of God even though we are left limping from the struggle between love and violence, blessing and curse, that is evident throughout the biblical narrative. To be a thinking Christian is to be a limping Christian, to say, along with Jacob, to the God we wrestle with, "Please, tell me your name."

This is an important question, for it determines who it is that we worship, whom it is that we surrender our lives to. The name of God matters. To simply say "God" brings complexity and numerous challenges, for we each make God in our own image, and, in doing so, the word *God* can often mean vastly different things to different people. As we gaze into the long and complex spectacle of Christian history alone, what we mean when we say "God" can

---

8. Below I will explore this idea of God having "two sides," and offer, I hope, a better reading than the love/holiness divide.

9. A detailed exploration of Acts 5, and its similarities to Josh 7, will follow below.

Introduction

lead us to very different traditions and theological perspectives. So when we approach the biblical text, the primary question we ask ourselves is, "*Who is it that we encounter when we encounter 'God' within it?*" To put it slightly differently, when we read the text we are asking two theological questions, as John Colwell so brilliantly summarized it: "What kind of God?" and "So what?"[10] In other words, who we believe God to be (or not to be) directly determines our ethics. Reflecting upon human history, these beliefs (or unbeliefs) about God, and what those beliefs (or unbeliefs) look like, have resulted in violence and murder across human culture. Now, of course, not all wars and violence are the direct result of religion, and, as recent studies have highlighted, only 7 percent of all the wars fought have been classified as stemming from a religious cause.[11] Indeed, as David Bentley Hart points out,

> by the end of the 20th century, wars had been waged on a scale never before imagined, and a number of Utopian, strictly secularist ideologies—each in its own way the inheritor both of the Enlightenment project to remake society on a more rational model and of the late 19th century project to "correct" human nature through the mechanisms of a provided state—had together managed to kill perhaps 150 million persons.... By century's end, all certainties had been shattered: the power of "organized religion" in the West had been largely subdued, but organized irreligion had proved a far more despotic, capricious and murderous historical force.[12]

Violence is a human problem, something we are very, very good at, a problem that transcends religion, creed, wealth, and nationality. We know *we* are violent, but what about the God of history, the one whom Christians worship as Father, Son, and Spirit? Has God revealed God's self to us within the biblical text as one of light and darkness, violence "the dark side of his blessing"? Or is the violence ascribed to God within the text simply a projection of our

---

10. Colwell, *Promise and Presence*, 1.
11. See Lurie, "Is Religion the Cause?"
12. Hart, *Story of Christianity*, 329–30.

INTRODUCTION

human violence, the human justification for our violent ways? Or is there more to the text, greater light that can be shone, that helps us understand what these violent texts are revealing?

Within the scope of this book I will try to answer these questions, beginning specifically with the story of Achan found in chapter 7 of the book of Joshua. I believe Achan's story—both in the run-up to his death and the aftermath—reveal significant insights into the way the story and culture of the Israelites can be understood. Not only that, but it is my contention that Achan's story, and the aftermath of those events, open up for us significant insights into who the God of Jesus of Nazareth is for us today. Indeed, nailing my colors to the mast straight away, I will go as far as to say that *sacrifice was never commanded by God*, and that what we discover within the biblical text is a God of total nonviolence, who, in the death and resurrection of Jesus, revealed that sacred violence has never existed; we are the ones who are violent, never God. But I don't believe we should throw away the text, cutting it apart according to our whims and desires. The text is telling us something important, and we need to wrestle with it to find out who God actually is. I believe there is a way of reading Scripture that is theologically coherent, that takes the biblical text seriously, and reveals Christ to us.

Along this journey we will also visit the fifth chapter of Acts, the story of Ananias and Sapphira, its impact upon the early Christian church, and the way their story reflects Achan's. But before we arrive at Achan, we need to start in the twentieth century and the hermeneutical grid through which I will be interpreting Scripture. I want to be absolutely clear and forthright about this from the very beginning. It is important that we are each honest as to our interpretive lens, the way we each come to Scripture according to our own bias, tradition, and theological convictions. There is no such thing as a "plain reading" of the Bible. None of us exist within a vacuum; we are all a product of our time and culture, living and breathing interpreters, reading ourselves into the text. However much we might strive to interpret the Bible without prejudice, it is simply an impossible task. Therefore, the honest approach is to

INTRODUCTION

recognize your own theological prejudices, and lean into Scripture with confidence in those convictions. Whether you are Reformed, progressive, evangelical, Lutheran, Baptist, Pentecostal, Catholic, Orthodox, or whatever, you read Scripture within that framework (or a mixture of traditions) and believe (consciously or unconsciously) this interpretive grid to be the most faithful to the biblical text. As is clear from Christian history, there is much debate as to which tradition, and which theological convictions, understand the biblical text best.[13]

So, as an act of full disclosure, I will begin with outlining the scapegoat theory by the French anthropologist and literary theorist René Girard, using this theory as the hermeneutical grid through which we interpret the story of Achan and the biblical text. I will offer alternatives to this Girardian reading, and will show why such alternatives are unable to lead us to the Trinitarian God. Then, comparing Achan's story to the crucifixion, I will contest that the crucified Jesus of Nazareth was the forgiving victim, revealing a *God of nonviolence*, who, through his death, breaks the human cycle of violence, and shows us how we might live as a people who follow the way of peace.

It will be my contention throughout that this reading is not only fully faithful to the Bible as a whole but is also faithful to the God of history as revealed through Jesus, and gives us the ethical tools, by the Spirit, to witness today to this God as good news within our communities.

---

13. There is a lot of nostalgia regarding Christian history, a belief that "once upon a time" the church had a clear and developed theology, a theology that got distorted through the centuries. The truth of the matter is that the church has believed and debated those beliefs throughout its entire existence.

1

The Scapegoat

All those moments will be lost in time, like tears in rain.
Roy Batty, *Blade Runner*[1]

René Girard (1923–2015) was a French literary critic and social theorist who developed the theory of the scapegoat,[2] that all violence can be traced back to the system of *mimesis* (imitation) and mimetic conflict (I'll unpack these terms in a moment).

Girard argues that the Bible is a "text in travail,"[3] that within it we encounter both the voice of religion and revelation. To put it another way, the Bible contains both the voice of Jesus, who speaks peace, and the voice of "the satan" or accuser, who speaks violence. Or to put it differently again, the Bible contains the words of God, and the words of our own violent ways—the way we murder one another and ascribe it to the gods, the way we bring accusation to others in order to justify our violence against them.

Humanity, since its beginning, according to Girard's hypothesis, has always been violent, spiraling into ever escalating models of retaliation and conflict. The only way, according to Girard, that

---

1. Scott, *Blade Runner*.
2. See Girard, *Things Hidden*, 3–178.
3. Girard, "Generative Scapegoating," 141.

humanity did not wipe itself out was through the discovery of the "scapegoat." This person or people, the scapegoat, were chosen, usually at random, but based upon their oddness within society; a person upon whom community disintegration, conflict, and lack of peace is blamed. Once the community was united in their condemnation of the "scapegoat," that person was murdered in what Girard calls "the founding murder." The "scapegoat" needed to be someone whom no one will seek to avenge, and that everyone can blame, so that there are no repercussions. Furthermore, the innocence of the victim needs to be suppressed, as does the chance nature of their selection, so myths were created surrounding the victim as to their guilt, violence, and cause of violent disharmony among the community. The scapegoat has to be regarded as strange, odd, and odious, an object of hatred and condemnation; it was important that they were not seen to be "one of us," otherwise the myth would untangle, but, conversely, they needed to be enough like us to justify the arbitrary nature of their selection. Yet in their death a miracle occurs: peace is restored. The group or community cannot perceive that it was their own murderous mimetic rivalry and so, in a paradoxical twist, attribute the resulting peace to the victim. Here, argues Girard, is the origin of the gods of religion, myth, sacrifice, and ritual.

Myth arises to conceal the murder of the victim. This murder must not be seen as a murder, for if it was then the bewitching power of the process would become invalidated. It is also important to note that mimesis and scapegoating happen within the community at an entirely subconscious level. No one is aware of what is being played out, only the belief that the chaos and disintegration of the community is somebody's fault. Thus, the community projects onto the gods divine necessity for blood to bring peace. So powerful is the myth, and the collective condemnation of the victim, that the victims themselves can sometimes come to believe the lie. They can even offer themselves to "the gods" in order to restore peace to the community, believing that the offer of their own blood is the only way the favor of the gods can be restored. At first glance we might believe such beliefs are archaic nonsense, the result of primitive people who did not understand the true nature of the world. But only a cursory glance into modern history and we realize such beliefs are very much with us. From the Jewish Shoah to current immigration policies across the world, the belief that certain people are the cause of the community's or nation's problems continues to be a powerful poison that people drink. The "god" in these cases is always nationalism, and that a nation is being dishonored, failed, and disintegrating beneath immigration. The myth of scapegoating ensues to restore pride, cleanse the land, and return the nation to its former glory and "pure" identity;[4] through blood, "sins" are forgiven. Back to Girard's theory.

The violence and conflict that has arisen within the community now finds its totality vented out upon a victim that unites them in a common purpose and goal. Whereas previously the community was in chaos and disharmony, tearing itself apart through rivalry and undifferentiation (see below), now it is united in its murder of the victim. The killing of the scapegoat restores peace for the time being. Chaos has been subdued, and the group can now slowly become something that we would call "community." Killing the scapegoat becomes an act of life for the community, not an act of murder, an act of salvation rather than condemnation.

The scapegoat mechanism is characterized by the following elements.[5]

1. Mimetic Desire

Humanity, since our earliest days, is defined, in large part, by learning from, copying, and imitating others. We imitate each other—this is what the word *mimesis* means—by desiring and wanting each other's desires and wants. This is not actually a bad

---

4. For instance, in seeking to restore the pride of the German *Volk*, Hitler wanted to see a time "when a nation of citizens would arise which would be welded together through a common love and a common pride that would be invincible and indestructible forever." Hitler, *Mein Kampf*, 387.

5. Here I use and adapt Walter Wink's and Raymond Schwager's definitions of the scapegoat mechanism, alongside my own definition in *The Ghost of Perfection*. See Haward, *Ghost of Perfection*, 42–45; Wink, *Engaging the Powers*, 145–46; Schwager, *Must There Be Scapegoats?*, 46–47.

thing, as we learn how to speak, walk, and hopefully respect and care for our fellow humanity through imitation and the positive actions and behavior of others.

2. Mimetic Rivalry

Conflict eventually arises, however. The person or people we imitate often and easily become our rival because we want what they want, desire what they have, and seek in some way to *be* them. Someone then becomes the object of our hostility and violence. Think about how toddlers, when in a room full of toys, just want the one toy: every child in that room then wants that one toy. It is the desire created through the fact that someone else desires it: subject, model/rival, object; the triangle of desire.

3. The Crisis of Distinctions

We are all different, but those differences diminish as we desire the same thing. The social distinctions that order society and preserve peace, collapse. Since humanity has a natural tendency toward violence, this is the method we use to solve the crisis. Zombies are a great modern parable that illustrate the collapse of distinctions into a collective violence of shared desire. So we seek a scapegoat. What we are not consciously aware of is how the conflict can be averted if a scapegoat can be found.

4. The Necessary Victim

The identity of the scapegoat is not important. All that matters is that they are an "other." However, the scapegoat has to be enough like us in some way so that we have a sense of affiliation—we need to feel like they deserve it—yet different enough so that we do not feel guilty. The fact the hostilities cease after their death confirms to us their inherent guilt, and "new spheres of relative peace are created."[6]

5. Sacralizing the Victim

---

6. Haward, *Ghost of Perfection*, 46.

The victim becomes an object of curse, yet, paradoxically, they are also seen as sacred through their ability to bring peace to the community. The victim is then given special status, even divinity, as a result. Here, then, is the emergence of taboo, myth, and ritual.

6. Sacrificial Repetition

Strictly controlled scenarios of sacrifice are now instituted involving ritual and myth, prohibitions and laws. These sacrifices happen with regularity to ensure, "internal aggressions are thus diverted once again to the outside, and the community is saved from self-destruction."[7]

Religion covers up the sacrificial mechanism by means of myth, ritual, and prohibition. It institutionalizes amnesia regarding the origins of violence, and endows violence with an aura of necessity and divine ordination that disguises its cost to the victims. Kierkegaard puts it like this:

> The ethical expression for what Abraham did is, that he would murder Isaac; the religious expression is, that he would sacrifice Isaac.[8]

This, however, is the uniqueness of some of the biblical story, but especially the Gospels, in that the story that we are invited to hear is from the view of the victim, the one being scapegoated or sacrificed. Girard argues that in ancient texts we only hear the story from the victor, never the victim, whereas the Scriptures offer us moments where the victim is heard. As we journey through the biblical narrative, we increasingly hear the voice of the victim, the cries from the victim's perspective, not entirely covered up by myth. Once we arrive at Jesus, the full view of the innocence of the victim is on display, and we see a God who calls for peace not killing, forgiveness not vengeance.[9] John Calvin (1509–1564) writes,

---

7. Haward, *Ghost of Perfection*, 47.
8. Kierkegaard, *Fear and Trembling*, 41.
9. "He has exhorted us to lead all men, by patience and gentleness, from shame and the love of evil. And this indeed is proved in the case of many who . . . have changed their violent and tyrannical disposition." Justin Martyr, *First Apology*, 16.

> Since the beginning of the world there has been no region, no city, in short no household, that could not do without religion, there lies in this a tacit confession of a sense of deity inscribed in the hearts of all.[10]

Calvin is on to something here, and Girard helps bring to clarity what Calvin does not quite see, namely, that sacred violence is what humanity "could not do without." Ancient communities tore a victim apart in order to stop them tearing themselves apart. "Inscribed in the hearts of all" has been our need for sacred violence, and it is this "sense of deity" that humanity has been offering victims to "since the foundation of the world."[11] We desire sacrifice to bring us a fragile peace, and we ascribe it to the gods. And in a world of militarism, greed, and racism, not much seems to have changed.

All of this above thus serves us as a means to interpret Achan's story. It is my contention that reading the story of Achan through the hermeneutical lens of scapegoat theory provides us with a remarkable insight and perspective on this text, enabling us to *hear the voice of Jesus of Nazareth within this text.* I am not for one moment suggesting this is the only way of reading Scripture, but I do believe that this is an interpretation that enables us to read Scripture in a way that is faithful to the nonviolent ethic of Jesus, and thus to hold a nonviolent theology of God.

---

10. Calvin, *Institutes*, 1.3.1.
11. Matt 13:35.

2

The Cry of Achan

No live organism can continue to exist sanely under conditions of absolute reality.

STEVEN CRAIN, *THE HAUNTING OF HILL HOUSE*[1]

WE ENCOUNTER ACHAN IN the book of Joshua, chapter 7. The victory of Jericho in chapter 6[2] and the declaration that "the LORD was with Joshua"[3] still rings out. The story of Achan follows after a great victory, the favor of God still with the Israelites. Notice how the community is in harmony, a community united in its victory over Jericho and the belief that it exists within divine blessing. The Israelites have experienced great disharmony and crisis at various points since their deliverance from Egypt, so this sense of blessing must not be underestimated within Girard's hypothesis; this harmony exists because of the community's recent violent victory

---

1. Flanagan, *Haunting of Hill House.*
2. "So the people shouted, and the trumpets were blown. As soon as the people heard the sound of the trumpets, they raised a great shout, and the wall fell down flat, so the people charged straight ahead into the city and captured it. Then they devoted to destruction by the edge of the sword all in the city, both men and women, young and old, oxen, sheep, and donkeys." Josh 6:20–21 (NRSV).
3. Josh 6:27a (NRSV).

over Jericho, united together in their elimination of those that pose a threat to their existence.

Girard asserts that "violence . . . initially decomposes communities and subsequently recomposes them, thanks to the unanimous scapegoating triggered by the decomposition."[4] He continues,

> Because our desires are mimetic, they resemble each other and cluster together in systems of opposition that are obstinate . . . and contagious. This is how scandals come to be. As they become fewer and bigger, scandals plunge communities into crises that are inflamed more and more. The inflammation reaches the crucial moment when unanimous convergence of the community against a single victim results in a total scandal, the "abscess of fixation" that pacifies the violence and puts together again the harmony that was torn apart.[5]

Here Girard is highlighting the extreme uniting power violence has upon a community, the way, when focused upon a victim, it can radically "recompose" a group, bringing them together within a common purpose and cause. Although the violence stems initially from a breakdown in the social cohesion, and then is displayed through radically disruptive means—violence is always disruptive—it works as a social glue, joining a community through its act.

Because Achan has taken some of the "devoted things"[6] from the spoils of war, the Lord's anger burns against the Israelites; this is the set-up, by the writer, as to why the unfolding crisis occurs. As the reader we are left in no doubt as to why the attempt to capture Ai goes wrong, and why "the hearts of the people melted and turned to water."[7] We are told it is all Achan's fault. The text invites us to be united in time and space in condemnation of Achan, to belong to those who recognize his guilt, and therefore agree with his punishment.

---

4. Girard, *I See Satan*, 182.
5. Girard, *I See Satan*, 94.
6. Josh 7:1 (NRSV).
7. Josh 7:5 (NRSV).

In verse 10 God tells Joshua that the reason for their defeat is that the Israelites have sinned and taken some of the devoted things, stolen from God, acted deceitfully, and, by taking the devoted things, have "become a thing devoted for destruction themselves."[8] The emergence of "prohibition" within the text is significant; the things devoted to God for destruction were those very things that create rivalry and desire within the community, and thus, according to Girard's theory, the possibility for "contagion" of desire, rivalry, thus violence. Notice that Joshua warns the people to "keep away from the things devoted to destruction,[9] so as not to covet and take any of the devoted things and make the camp of Israel an object for destruction, bringing trouble upon it."[10]

With desire (to covet) comes rivalry.

> The desire prohibited by the tenth commandment must be the desire of all human beings—in other words, simply desire as such. . . . We tend to desire what our neighbor has or what our neighbor desires. If individuals are naturally inclined to desire what their neighbors possess, or to desire what their neighbors even simply desire, this means that rivalry exists at the very heart of human social relations. This rivalry, if not thwarted, would permanently endanger the harmony and even the survival of all human communities. Rivalistic desires are all the more overwhelming since they reinforce one another. The principle of reciprocal escalation and one-upmanship governs this type of conflict. This phenomenon is so common, so well-known to us, and so contrary to our concept of ourselves, thus so humiliating, that we prefer to remove it from our consciousness and act as if it did not exist. But all the while we know it does exist.[11]

With mimetic rivalry comes lack of distinctions, our differences consumed by our common desire that in turn leads to chaos and violence within the community, threatening its very existence.

---

8. Josh 7:12b (NRSV).
9. See below for further discussion around interpretations of *herem*.
10. Josh 6:18 (NRSV).
11. Girard, *I See Satan*, 8–9.

What I mean by this is that when a community becomes "undifferentiated" through its common desire, rivalry breaks out because our desires all imitate one another. We see it all the time on social media as microaggressions escalate through this contagion of shared desire. Humanity has always desired as rivals, and the prohibition on the Israelites in regard to the devoted things is an attempt at limiting desire. Or, to put it according to the biblical text, will make the Israelite community *herem*.

Devoted to Destruction

Douglas Earl argues that *herem* is best interpreted within the context of the book of Joshua as obedience to covenant with YHWH. "Covenant violation is really the issue," argues Earl, highlighting how the presence of *herem* objects symbolize covenant violation, and to restore obedience to the covenant with YHWH is through destruction of *herem*. Therefore, according to Earl, the story of Achan can be interpreted through covenant violation, and how the "concern of the story is that of identity construction with respect to the covenant; the covenant, and obedience to it, is central to the characterization of Israel's identity." It is, he goes on, "a story as a 'limit-situation' that disobedience to the covenant makes one an outsider, symbolized by death of the offender and their family."[12] Joel Kaminsky, however, interprets *herem* according to contagion, as that which contaminates and defiles the community. He argues that when one "misappropriates" *herem* objects, they "run the risk of having the tabooed status" of the *herem* transferred to themselves. Kaminsky goes on,

> This is wholly analogous to the contagiousness of the state of impurity, and a provision of the law of impurity is really the best commentary on the story of Achan's crime. . . . [*Herem*] can spread and thus can be described as something that is contagious.[13]

---

12. Earl, "Reading Joshua," 94.
13. Kaminsky, "Joshua," 331–32.

Therefore, according to this reading, Achan's crime contaminates the whole Israelite community, a contagion of taboo that spreads without prejudice. Earl believes it is a category mistake to interpret *herem* in this way, arguing that Deuteronomy highlights how it is the practice of idolatry, and the "clinging to" *herem* objects, rather than "clinging to" YHWH, that is the actual problem; the forsaking of God as king is the issue.

Herem, then, can be interpreted in a variety of ways, with some translators opting for "utterly destroy," "devote," "ban," or "separate." The NRSV translates *herem* in Josh 6:18 as "things devoted to destruction," and, as we have seen with Earl and Kaminsky, there are further nuances and challenges to these interpretations. However, if we follow Girard (and Augustine) in that *misplaced desire* is our greatest threat, then it is possible to interpret *herem* as *a problem of desire*.

Herem as destruction, contagion, idolatry, covenant violation, ban, and to separate can, in each instance, be understood through the lens of desire, desire of that which must be *destroyed* to eliminate desires, and thus eliminate violent rivalry within the community. Therefore, if we continue to interpret *herem* through the lens of mimetic desire, it could also be interpreted as that which brings the *contagion* of violence *through* such desire. Or, as that which brings *idolatry*, a "clinging to" *herem* rather than YHWH because the community's desires are utterly misplaced, thus creating the possibility of mimetic rivalry. It could also be seen as that which brings *covenant violation*, the rejection of that which suppresses rivalry through the strict obedience to ritual and taboo, and as that which is *banned and to be separated from*, thus removing desire and rivalry from the community; if covenant with God—and *imitation of* God—is the highest goal, then *herem* objects can violate that covenant and godly imitative relationship.

It is important at this point to note that while the objects of *herem* will be the vehicle through which guilt is assigned to Achan, that vehicle of guilt could have been any perceived violation; what matters most is that a scapegoat is found through the act of collective blame.

Back to Achan. God orders Joshua, tribe by tribe, clan by clan, household by household, one by one, to find the guilty person. The following day Joshua does as God commands, until Achan is left. A question we should ask of the text is, if God knew it was Achan, why did God not simply tell Joshua it was Achan? It would have been simple for God to tell Joshua that Achan did it, yet a long and elaborate process takes place instead. Why? According to a Girardian reading, because the selection of Achan was not a divine order but the necessary arbitrary selection of a scapegoat.

Now, here, I have to admit that there is nothing *obvious* in the text that highlights why Achan is chosen as the scapegoat before the discovery of the treasures, no sense of his "otherness" prior to his selection. That he has treasure is actually irrelevant because it is likely many of the families had found and hidden treasure. Achan's selection has something to do with another kind of "otherness" that is not readily available within the text. However, we could *tentatively* suggest his lineage is the "otherness" needed: Achan is the son of Carmi, son of Zabdi, son of Zerah; Zerah was a twin.[14] Why is that possibly significant? Girard makes the assertion that within ancient cultures twins were regarded as a curse, a cause of crisis, precisely because they are a double, and there is a strong fear of anything within these cultures of that which can create mimetic rivalry; twins were regarded as contagious in many ancient cultures because of the inevitable rivalry and violence that resulted from their nondifferentiation.[15] Put differently, if our undifferentiation creates rivalry, and then violence, twins represent a significant danger. In Plato's *Symposium*, Aristophanes speaks of how humans were created with two faces and four legs. Zeus, in seeking to better control humanity, divided them in two. Perhaps, within some traditions, twins represent the fear that humans have found a way to be joined together again, and so rediscover an ancient power that will disrupt the power of the gods? Speaking personally as an identical twin, we were always regarded as the same growing up, identified by family and friends as "twin." Although a novelty

14. See Gen 38:27–30, Josh 7:1.
15. See Girard, *Things Hidden*, 142.

at first, our closeness become a cause of contention with others as they were unable to be part of our world in the same way. It was as though our relationship was regarded as a threat to others; mimetic rivalry, the desire to have our relationship. Perhaps it simply highlighted the inadequacies in their own relationships, and thus they vented their own dissatisfaction upon my brother and me. Our bond has enabled us to navigate significant personal challenges, strengthened by the relationship we share together.[16] It is a guess as to whether Achan's history of twins within his own family line caused him to be viewed with suspicion, yet I suggest it is quite plausible.

Nonetheless, the opening verse of the seventh chapter of Joshua makes it clear that there is no doubt to the writer and the community of Achan's "otherness" in light of his perceived crime; it has been decided that Achan clearly is the problem. The random selection of the scapegoat needs only a sense of "otherness," whatever that otherness is, and Joshua found in Achan the perfect victim, a selection affirmed through what he had taken.

When mimetic rivalry breaks out within a community, the selection of the scapegoat has to be condoned by the whole community, and so the way Joshua picks Achan out creates a community event, led by God's chosen leader, thus giving it a sense of divine approval. In reality much of the community may well have taken "the devoted things" for themselves (human nature), and so in choosing Achan the chances were that he, like many others, had silver and gold hidden, because probability combined with desire for riches will lead to fairly obvious results. But a myth is created around Achan's singular guilt in order to maintain what we could call the "divine necessity" for his death. Quite simply, the defeat at Ai, and the fear now sweeping through the Israelite camp, is all placed upon Achan. As Girard points out,

> The victim is held responsible for the crisis. . . . The experience of disorder and the return to order, for which such a victim is made responsible constitute an experience

---

16. For a personal account of our relationship, particularly around the issue of depression and mental health, see Haward, "Twin Speaks," 186–97.

too intolerable and incomprehensible for rational understanding.... This knowledge will then take precedence over all else.... It is logical to think that the terrifying aspect of the epiphany is designed to impress in all hearts and minds the rules that the deity wants established.[17]

Such is the power of the stories around prohibition, taboo, and divine blessing that Achan readily accepts his guilt. As a result, Achan and his whole family, and all that he possesses, are taken by Joshua and all of Israel, stoned to death, and burned (Josh 7:24). Notice again the *collective nature* of violent punishment, something performed by the whole community to Achan and his family. It is worth hearing an extended quote of Girard here as to the significance of the collective act of murder done by the community to the victim.

> The community affirms its unity in the sacrifice, a unity that emerges from the moment when division is most intense.... But suddenly the opposition of everyone against everyone else is replaced by the opposition of all against one.... There is now the simplicity of a single conflict: the entire community on one side, and on the other, the victim. The nature of this sacrificial resolution is not difficult to comprehend; the community finds itself unified once more at the expense of a victim who is not only incapable of self-defense but is also unable to provoke any reaction of vengeance; the immolation of such a victim would never create fresh conflict or augment the crisis, since the victim has unified the community in its opposition.... In certain sacrifices the victim becomes an object of such hostility one must believe that it and it alone has been held responsible for the entire mimetic crisis.[18]

It is of vital importance that the whole community is involved in Achan's murder, for it justifies the myth surrounding his guilt, and also means no one person can be blamed for his death. More than this, however, it provides the cathartic release of crisis, fear, rage,

17. Girard, *Things Hidden*, 40–41.
18. Girard, *Things Hidden*, 24.

The Cry of Achan

and violence needed for the whole community to restore peace and order. In this community act the community tears apart a victim in order to rescue it from tearing itself apart through mimetic rivalry.

After Achan and his family have been killed a "great heap of stones"[19] are raised over them, a reminder to the community of what happens when that which is prohibited is transgressed, and to further remind the community, albeit unconsciously, of the power of scapegoating and sacrifice. The imagery and power of "stones" will play an important part in the unfolding narrative after Achan's death, a narrative that will be vital in our understanding of Christ's own death and resurrection. Let's unpack this idea a little further.

---

19. Josh 7:26 (NRSV).

3

Monuments of Murder

There are always consequences . . . and tonight, you are consequential.
VERNA, *The Fall of the House of Usher*[1]

IN A SHORT SPACE of time the book of Joshua recounts three events that result in stones being raised by the community. The first, for the purposes of our study, is the cairn of stones that are the lasting symbol of the act of the community against Achan and his family, *the monument of murder* we might say.

> Joshua said, "Why did you bring trouble on us? The LORD is bringing trouble on you today." And all Israel stoned him to death; they burned them with fire, cast stones on them, and raised over him a great heap of stones that remains to this day. Then the LORD turned from his burning anger. (Josh 7:25–26 NRSV)

Imagine the frenzied attack that is inevitable when a community unites in its condemnation against the victim, and the resulting heap of stones piled high, a lasting memorial of the community's perceived sense of divine justice. But for such an attack to take

---

1. Flanagan, *Fall of the House of Usher*.

place, people must be united in their condemnation, and brave enough to cast the stones.

When Jesus calls upon those "without sin be the first to cast a stone,"[2] he is not simply highlighting the sinfulness of us all, and the impact our own failings then have upon our capacity to judge; Jesus is also emphasizing how difficult it actually is to cast the first stone. It is no small thing to instigate someone's death, to be the first to take the first murderous step in calling down deathly judgment. However, once that first stone is cast, then a mimetic contagion will take place, everyone imitating the first "model," throwing their stones with a confidence only moments earlier they would never have possessed.[3] It is far easier for us to imitate the actions of the crowd than to step away and refuse its powerful dynamic. The mob dynamic makes involvement considerably more attractive, and less dangerous, than being uninvolved.

Once the stones have been cast it then becomes undemanding for the crowd to invent stories about the victim, justifying their actions against an enemy who "brought it on themselves," a person who was guilty of a crime that could not be ignored. We see how effectively such myth stories work in Achan's example, his guilt and judgment declared just by God, the leaders, the community, and even himself: "And Achan answered Joshua, 'It is true; I am the one who sinned against the Lord God of Israel.'"[4] As soon as a victim can be found upon whom everybody agrees is deserving of guilt—not for rational reasons but because of a mimetic tidal wave against them—a cathartic outpouring of peace sweeps across the

2. John 8:7.

3. To speak here of "possession" is, perhaps, wholly appropriate. I will unpack below ideas around Satan, but for now it is worth saying that crowds can be "possessed" by a murderous spirit. Now, I do not believe such a spirit is a legion of demons, but I am comfortable in saying that what occurs is "demonic." What I mean by this is an energy captivates the crowd that is committed to the singular goal of destruction, taking over previously rational people, and enabling them to commit acts they would never normally have considered. "Road rage" is another good example, where people are so overtaken by the extremity of anger (and mimetic rivalry—"this bit of road is mine"), they become murderous in their actions.

4. Josh 7:20 (NRSV).

people. This act of violence purges the community of its perceived impurities, like an antidote to poison.

The King of Ai

The next stone passage is after Achan's death when Joshua leads the Israelites into victory against the king of Ai, turning the city and all who lived there into "a desolate place."[5] It is no coincidence that this battle victory occurs immediately after Achan's death. The community have been united in their act of murder, bound together in the contagion of violence. This unanimity brings with it a remarkable strength and power, the belief of divine favor. Remember, before Achan's death the community was distressed by anxiety, confusion, and trouble.[6] But at the death of Achan a "miracle" occurs, and the community is galvanized, strengthened in their belief that God is with them. This is how scapegoating works; it binds the community together as the act of murder serves to cathartically release them from fear. Scapegoating is effective because it absorbs the fear of the community, taking the wrath of the community and releasing it onto the victim. As a result, peace is restored, however fragile such a peace might be. The city of Ai stood little chance against this united and reinvigorated community.

The king of Ai is hanged until evening, his body taken down, and then a cairn raised over it, the author of the text noting its lasting presence.

> And he hanged the king of Ai on a tree until evening, and at sunset Joshua commanded, and they took his body down from the tree, threw it down at the entrance of the gate of the city, and raised over it a great heap of stones, which stands there to this day. (Josh 8:29 NRSV)

---

5. Josh 8:28 (NRSV).
6. "Why did you bring trouble on us? The LORD is bringing trouble on you today." Josh 7:25 (NRSV).

Immediately after this episode Joshua builds an altar to Yahweh, an altar of "undressed stones that no iron tool had ever worked."[7] Here we have *significant textual perspicuity*: on this *stone* altar sacrifices are made to God. Its purpose, through sacrificial repetition, to mirror the violence, and thus re-stabilize the community. This community has known the destabilizing effects that result from the transgression of laws, the violation of prohibition. Sacrifice acts as a means of re-stabilizing the community. First we have the stoning of Achan, each stone used to *kill the victim*; then we have the dead body of the king of Ai, each stone used to *cover the victim*; then we have the altar, each stone used to *establish the need for a victim*.

This is how scapegoating works: kill the victim; cover the act in myth; establish rituals to maintain the act. Therefore, in these sacrifices, as Joshua reestablished the act of sacrifice, the community *reasserts its identity*.

> Israel seems for the moment to have restored its traditional system of animal sacrifice and thereby to have recaptured its religious poise.[8]

See how the ritual of sacrifice immediately follows the act of scapegoating Achan and his family? It is vital for the survival of the community that strict rituals, (unconsciously) imitating the murder of Achan, are followed and adhered to. The cohesion and peace that resulted from stoning Achan and his family, and then murdering the people of Ai, must be continually channeled in order to maintain peace. This can only happen through repeated sacrificial offerings.

The stones heaped upon Achan and his family, and the king of Ai, mirror the altar that Joshua builds, an altar of undressed stones that serves to remind the community of the power and necessity of sacrifice to stabilize the community from chaos. The death of Achan helps reestablish ritual sacrifice within the community. Of course, the community does not consciously recognize its actions for what they are, and it is important for the myth and practice of

---

7. Josh 8:31 (NRSV).
8. Bailie, *Violence Unveiled*, 165.

scapegoating that they do not perceive what is happening, for in doing so would render it useless.

Girard says that sacrificial stones mark the foundation of ancient cities, stones that have a direct link with stories of lynching, hidden under the myths and rituals that these stones now represent.[9] Community is established through these acts of murder. Society springs forth through these ancient acts of lynching. That the stone is removed from the tomb of Jesus is, then, revelatory.

The cairn of stones that is raised to remain over Achan, and the king of Ai, reminds the community of its unanimity in judgment, the restoration of "divine blessing" in purging sin from the land; the stones that were heaped high remain, thus affirming that their murder is regarded as necessary and sacred. Achan's death is considered by the community as a divine command, the stoning and resulting cairn a reminder that the voice and actions of the community are the voice and actions of God against the guilty. At the resurrection of Jesus, however, *the stone is removed*, exposing the scapegoating mechanism that humanity has engaged in from time immemorial. The removal of the stone from the tomb is the sign that God has removed all "cairns" and refused to allow the community to raise a monument of murder against the Son. As we shall see, the removal of the stone from the tomb is God's active word, by the Spirit, declaring that God has no place within the sacrificial system, that the scapegoating of a victim is a human act, the stone altars of history the remnants of human violence seeking divine justification.

The stones raised over Achan and his family help to justify the community in its act of killing, that peace has been restored. Yet the Son of God exposes this myth by the removal of the stone from his tomb, a tomb he occupies because of collective violence against him by the community. By removing the stone, the principle of sacrifice has been inverted and exposed by God. In other words, the stones heaped over Achan, indeed over all victims of scapegoating, speak of a community who believed in the divine approval of sacrifice, but the removal of the stone from Jesus's tomb

---

9. Girard, *Things Hidden*, 164.

speaks of a God who *was never involved*. Indeed, it declares God's judgment over sacrifice. We will get to this point shortly. However, before we explore this idea further, we're going on a detour to the story of Ananias and Sapphira in the fifth chapter of the book of Acts. As we shall see, there are remarkable parallels between this story in the life of the early church and the story of Achan. The unpacking of both will gives us ever more clarity in understanding exactly how Jesus inverts the principle of sacrifice, and transforms all of history toward the *eschatological telos of peace*.

4

Acts 5:1–11

We can make it together. But we can only make it together.
GLENN RHEE, *THE WALKING DEAD*[1]

GIRARD UNCOVERED THE MODEL of desire, and the act of scapegoating, in a variety of modern and ancient texts, including the Bible. He saw how a pattern of scapegoating emerged, regardless of when and where the story was being told. These patterns were the scapegoating process, and earlier we defined it as six stages.

1. Mimetic Desire.
2. Mimetic Rivalry.
3. The Crisis of Distinctions.
4. The Necessary Victim.
5. Sacralizing the Victim.
6. Sacrificial Repetition.

To explore the story of Ananias and Sapphira in light of scapegoat theory, we can distill the process into four elements: a crisis in the community, the selection of the scapegoat, the expulsion of the

1. Ramsay, *Walking Dead*.

scapegoat, and the (de)stabilized community.² Before we explore these four processes, let's remind ourselves of what the text in Acts actually says.

> But a certain man by the name of Ananias, together with his wife Sapphira, sold a piece of property, And he kept some of the proceeds for himself (his wife also being aware of this), and brought along a certain portion of it and placed it at the feet of the Apostles. But Peter said, "Ananias, why did the Accuser so fill your heart that you lie to the Spirit, the Holy One, and keep some of the proceeds from the land for yourself? So long as it remained unsold, did it not belong to you? And once sold was it not in your power? Why was such a deed put into your heart? You did not lie to men, but to God." And, on hearing these words, Ananias fell down and yielded up his soul; and great fear came over all who heard of it. And the young men rose and shrouded him and, carrying him out, buried him. Then an interval of about three hours elapsed and his wife, not knowing what had happened, came in. And Peter spoke aloud to her: "Tell me whether you sold the land for this much." And she said, "Yes, for this much." And Peter to her: "Why was it agreed between you to try the Spirit of the Lord? Look: at the door, the feet of those who have buried your husband; they will carry you out also." And at once she fell down at his feet and yielded up her soul; and, coming in, the young men found her dead and, carrying her out, buried her beside her husband. And great fear came over the entire assembly and over everyone hearing of these things. (Acts 5:1–11)

---

2. My thanks to many friends, in person and online, who, through years of discussions, helped me better process these ideas that follow, specifically in regard to Ananias and Sapphira.

Crisis in the Community

At first glance it would be easy to assume that there is no crisis within the community. This early Christian community, we are told, is of one spirit, sharing all things in common.

> And both the heart and the soul of the multitude of those who had come to have faith were one, and no one said that any of the possessions belonging to him was his own, but everything was owned among them communally. (Acts 4:32)

However, this "unity" is born from within a crisis, namely the attempts by the religious leaders and temple authorities to expel and persecute the Jerusalem Christians. What can initially be perceived as a state of unity is actually the church defining itself over and against another "tribe"; the language that emerges is of a *particular* persecution and attack, from a *particular* group who are against them—notice the parallels with the Israelites entering the promised land.

The temple leaders have arrested Peter and John, and make very specific threats.

> And, summoning them, they enjoined them not to speak or teach in the name of Jesus at all. But, in reply, Peter and John said to them, "Judge for yourselves whether it is upright before God to listen to you rather than to God; For we are unable not to speak of the things we have seen and heard." And they, having made additional threats, released them. (Acts 4:18–21a)

When Peter and John return to their Christian brothers and sisters, they make it clear where the threat of their survival is coming from.

> And now, Lord, consider their threats and grant it to your slaves to speak your word with all boldness, By stretching forth your hand so that healing and signs and wonders may occur through the name of your holy servant Jesus. (Acts 4:29–30)

So here in the text we have a clear tension between the religious leaders and this new Christian community. As we highlighted above in chapter 1, such tension is a result of mimetic conflict, where simultaneous desire—for religious authority, power, religious truth—and resulting rivalry break out. It is also important to note the role *positive* mimesis has within the new church, as the sharing of money and possessions and the redistribution of wealth was actively pursued by many within the church. Yet this positive mimetic action is double-edged with mimetic rivalry, as *not* giving all your possessions to the church becomes a reason for expulsion; there is a call to imitate the generosity of everyone else, or face the consequences.

There is also the implied sociological crisis that is present, namely, that there was a problem of poverty within the wider community, highlighted by the redistribution of wealth to those who were in need (Acts 4:35). There had to be a resolution to how the early Christian community provided for the poor now that the support of the traditional mechanisms of Jewish almsgiving were no longer available to this new sect. Following Jesus took away those mechanisms, no doubt leaving many families in desperate situations. The selling of goods and redistribution provided a solution, yet was it sustainable? And all of this is happening in a time of possible great scarcity for most people in the land. Scholars have argued that the itinerant lifestyle of Jesus might well have been because of loss of property and livelihood due to the harsh taxation that existed at the time. Peasant farmers would have made up much of the lower class as "first-century Galilee was mainly agricultural, with little fishing industry, and its population was economically strongly dependent on the wealthy elite, the majority of whom lived in Sepphoris and Tiberias, some even in Jerusalem."[3] Much of the community would likely have consumed everything they produced, with rents, taxes, loan repayments, and interest on top leaving nothing left to trade with.

---

3. Häkkinen, "Poverty," para. 2.

> The obvious difficulty with the city-state as a community, with its stress on mutual sharing of both burdens and benefits, was the hard fact that its members were unequal. The most troublesome inequality was not between town and country, not between classes, but simply between rich and poor.[4]

Poverty and power struggles will thus create the crisis within the community that will feed the need for a scapegoat. Remember, when a community is in crisis, as we saw in Josh 6 and 7, then a scapegoat is sought in order to resolve the crisis: killing the scapegoat is an act of catharsis, whereby the wrath, fear, and violence of the community is expelled upon the victim.

The Selection of the Scapegoat

Ananias and Sapphira are chosen because of their perceived lies and greed, and are singled out by the community, much like Achan and his family. Girard makes it clear that scapegoats are usually selected—unconsciously—by some difference, whether it is a physical mark, disability, racial difference, or other such "oddities." And it is always random. In other words, there would be multiple people who would fit because of their physical appearance, or place within the community, but the scapegoat will be random, a chance happening where a particular person is chosen, and the community justify their selection through the placement of guilt upon them. It matters not whether the person or people have actually committed the crime they are accused of—to be a scapegoat is to bear the wrath of the crowd, regardless of innocence or guilt. Yet we are told so little about Ananias and Sapphira except that they are guilty. The only words the text allows us to hear from their mouths are from Sapphira when she answers Peter's question. The parallels with Achan's selection are obvious: the guilt of greed. More than that, the redistribution of wealth in the Jerusalem church acts in the same way as *herem* did in the Israelite community. Just as the

---

4. Finley, *Ancient Economy*, 152.

spoils of war were to be taken by the Israelites and put "into the treasury of the house of the LORD,"[5] so too were the early Christians compelled to sell their land and bring the profits to the feet of the disciples (Acts 4:34–35). Yet, like Achan, it is unlikely that Ananias and Sapphira were the only people to hold back some of their profits, so why were they singled out? Like Achan, we will never know.

And what of Peter's question to Sapphira, the only moment we hear either one of the couple speak? This, it appears to me, is an early example within the Christian church of how power and manipulation works within leadership. He uses the question only as a way for her to heap guilt upon herself, and thus condemn her, rather than finding a way to resolve the situation. It reads very much as a trap. Whereas Jesus sought to eliminate shame and restore each person's sense of "somebodiness," Peter reverts to humiliation and blame. Peter, it seems to me, wants to show his authority, and, in doing so, remind the community of who he is, and his position over them.

The Expulsion of the Scapegoat

A judgment of guilt is proclaimed loudly over the couple by Peter, with no room for ambiguity. It is interesting how the condemnation over both Ananias and Sapphira mirrors, not only Achan, but also Jesus.

> And the chief priest, tearing his tunics, says, "What need do we still have for witnesses? You heard the blasphemy. How does it seem to you?" And they all adjudged him to be liable to death. (Mark 14:63–65)

Peter's charge against the couple mirrors this charge of blasphemy, accusing them both of lying to the Spirit and withholding from God, parallels again with Achan. There is also a strong sense within the text that Peter is *imitating* his own betrayal, using Ananias and Sapphira as a scapegoat in order to continue the work

---

5. Josh 6:24 (NRSV).

of clearing his own conscience. Notice that this episode is framed entirely as a betrayal, the couple being asked a question outright that will prove their loyalty, yet both failing. Peter is engaged here in mimetic rivalry, his own experience of betrayal now shaping how he will respond to this couple within the church. Peter had every opportunity to handle the situation differently. Why did he not try to find a way for Ananias and Sapphira to remain included and part of this new community of believers? Jesus did not expel Peter but welcomed him in with forgiveness and a new charge of responsibility. But Peter chooses the path of scapegoating, mirroring the violence that he had witnessed happening to Jesus. Rather than recognizing—like Paul would—how scapegoating works, Peter is consumed by its power. This power will lead to, at the very least, expulsion,[6] and most likely, death.

The text tells us that Ananias and Sapphira both drop dead, but notice that the language used is falling down and *then* "yielding up" their souls. *Nowhere in the text does it say that God strikes them down.* Some commentators, like Stanley Hauerwas, have suggested that the news of their deceit being spoken out loud within the church community caused both Ananias and Sapphira to have heart attacks.[7] Yet the falling down, and then dying, suggests that they were attacked; the community grabs them (falling down), and then lynches them (yielding up their soul). The language of "dropping dead," from a Girardian hermeneutic, is important to consider.

Drop Dead

People apparently being struck down instantly by God doesn't actually happen that often in the Hebrew Scriptures. Certainly, there are many moments when we are told God's judgment comes violently against people and nations, but falling dead on the spot, like Ananias and Sapphira, is not very common. There are Nadab

---

6. Obviously, the text says the couple died, yet we must be open to the possibility they were expelled and sent away.

7. Hauerwas, *Matthew*, 174.

and Abihu, the sons of Aaron, who create impure fire in Leviticus;[8] Korah, and those he is with, in Numbers;[9] and Uzzah who steadies the ark in 2 Samuel.[10] All of these deaths happen in God's holy presence, a presence that was later believed to reside in the temple. And all of these deaths are to do with something going wrong with sacred ritual. This is key.

Through a Girardian understanding, sacred rituals channel the violence of the community, and, therefore, contain or hold back the outbreak of chaotic violence. In other words, the rituals are designed to maintain the peace of the community, and protect the community from violence, reminding them, unconsciously, of the power of the original sacrifice. Scapegoating happens when the laws and rituals are believed to have been transgressed. It is easy for a community to descend into an outburst of rage, turning their fear upon each other, or leaders of the community.

Now, according to the text (and remember how myths are often created to conceal the innocence of the victim), Ananias

---

8. "Now Aaron's sons Nadab and Abihu each took his censer, put fire in it, and laid incense on it, and they offered unholy fire before the Lord, such as he had not commanded them. And fire came out from the presence of the Lord and consumed them, and they died before the Lord. Then Moses said to Aaron, 'This is what the Lord meant when he said,

> "Through those who are near me
> I will show myself holy,
> and before all the people
> I will be glorified."'

And Aaron was silent." Lev 10:1–3 (NRSV).

9. "As soon as he finished saying all this, the ground under them split apart and the earth opened its mouth and swallowed them and their households, and all those associated with Korah, together with their possessions. They went down alive into the realm of the dead, with everything they owned; the earth closed over them, and they perished and were gone from the community. At their cries, all the Israelites around them fled, shouting, 'The earth is going to swallow us too!' And fire came out from the Lord and consumed the two hundred fifty men who were offering the incense." Num 16:31–35 (NRSV).

10. "When they came to the threshing floor of Nacon, Uzzah reached out his hand to the ark of God and took hold of it, for the oxen lurched. The anger of the Lord was kindled against Uzzah, and God struck him there, and he died there beside the ark of God." 2 Sam 6:6–7 (NRSV).

and Sapphira are guilty *according to the ethics and law of the early Christian church*. We might well, rightly, want to challenge the idea of their guilt (or not), but the text wants us to be in no doubt that they have transgressed the ethical boundaries imposed by the church. Ananias and Sapphira's deaths are related to an ethical transgression but could also be seen as a ritual transgression. The act of placing money at the disciple's feet echoes *herem*, and those things devoted to God. Peter's judgment invokes the language of God's *immediate and holy presence*, his role like that of a priest within the temple.

There is also the way the context of this passage feeds into Second Temple eschatology. Notice the prayer of the Jerusalem church that precedes the action of *positive* mimesis in the sharing of goods.

> And they, having listened, lifted their voices to God with one accord and said, "Master, you are he who made the sky and the land and the sea and all the things that are in them, Who spoke by a Holy Spirit through the mouth of your servant, our father David, saying, 'Why did the gentiles rage and the peoples devise vain intrigues? The kings of the earth drew up ranks and the rulers gathered together against the Lord and against his Anointed.' For in truth both Herod and Pilate, along with the gentiles and peoples of Israel, conspired in this city against your holy servant Jesus, whom you anointed, To do what your hand and your counsel designated should happen in advance; And now, Lord, consider their threats and grant it to your slaves to speak your word with all boldness, By stretching forth your hand so that healing and signs and wonders may occur through the name of your holy servant Jesus." (Acts 5:24–30)

This prayer significantly departs from the teachings of Jesus in the Gospels in his calling for blessing upon enemies, and the command to be peacemakers. The thrust of Christ's teaching is *nonrivalistic* and *nonviolent*. In other words, his life, as declared at his birth by the angels, is one of "peace," and "great joy" for "all people."[11]

11. See Luke 2:8–15.

Here, however, the church pit themselves as rivals *over and against everyone else*. It is a highly combative prayer that rhymes with Second Temple eschatology waiting for the enemies of God to be destroyed, with the expectation of a violent parousia.[12] Second Temple eschatology anticipated that the Messiah would return to slaughter the gentile occupants of the Holy Land and inhabit the temple again, executing judgment as it was believed he had done in former times. Achan's story is found embedded within the violent judgment of God against foreign nations. Such judgment was expected to continue during the time of Jesus. The vision of the messianic age that we find in places like the Enochite literature,[13] and others, is one of exclusivity and violent zeal. In contrast, Isaiah's vision of the great banquet of peace, in which both the Jews and the gentile nations will share together, proclaims,

> On this mountain the LORD of hosts will make for all peoples
> a feast of rich food, a feast of well-aged wines,
> of rich food filled with marrow, of well-aged wines strained clear.
>
> And he will destroy on this mountain
> the shroud that is cast over all peoples,
> the covering that is spread over all nations;
> he will swallow up death forever.
>
> Then the LORD God will wipe away the tears from all faces,
> and the disgrace of his people he will take away from all the earth,
> for the LORD has spoken. (Isa 25:6–8 NRSV)

---

12. The expectation, presence, coming, and arrival of the Messiah.

13. For example:

> And the word of his mouth slays all the sinners,
> And all the unrighteous are destroyed from before his face. . . .
>
> And they shall be terrified,
> And they shall be downcast of countenance,
> And pain shall seize them,
> When they see that Son of Man Sitting on the throne of his glory.
> (1 Enoch 62:2b, 5)

Charles, "Book of Enoch."

However, in Second Temple eschatology this is significantly changed. Only Jews who observe the Torah with absolute attention to detail will be admitted to this glorious feast, and, according to the Qumran Messianic Rule, "anyone smitten in the flesh, or paralyzed in the feet and hands, or lame, or blind or deaf or dumb or smitten in the flesh with a visible blemish," will be permanently excluded.[14] This exclusion is in stark contrast to the inclusiveness found in Christ, who declared, "And I, when I am lifted up from the earth, will drag everyone to me."[15]

Clearing of the Temple

The teachings and actions of Jesus subvert and deconstruct the entirety of sacrificial eschatology. The eschatological vision of Jesus is encountered through his so-called clearing of the temple.[16] Notice how John's Gospel frames the episode with the bold declaration from Jesus that if they destroyed the temple (his body), he would rebuild it in three days (his resurrection).[17]

Jesus is making a direct parallel of his action within the temple grounds to his own death.

So what is Jesus doing at this moment? When Jesus enters the temple, he overturns the tables of the money changers, and stops people from carrying "containers" or "vessels" (*skeuos* in Greek, see Mark 11:16) through the temple. This small detail is highly significant. In the Septuagint, (the Greek translation of the Hebrew Scriptures) the word *skeuos* is used in Lev 6 about earthenware vessels that carried sacrificial offerings: "A clay vessel [*skeuos*] in which it [the sacrificial offering] was boiled shall be broken."[18] This vessel contained sacrificial offerings, yet Jesus prevented people from bringing them through the temple. Jesus then drives the animals out of the temple using a stock whip (a *phragellion*, see John

14. See Bailey, *Jesus Through Middle Eastern Eyes*, 110–11.
15. John 12:32.
16. John 2:13–25.
17. See John 2:18–22.
18. Lev 6:28 (NRSV).

2:15), a braided or tied cord that was used *specifically* and *only* to herd animals. Jesus is not attacking people with a whip, but *removing the means of sacrifice.*

Jesus was shutting down the sacrificial system. By stopping sacrificial offerings and animals coming into the temple, Jesus was transforming the very idea and understanding of who God is. He would reveal, through his own death (temple) and resurrection (rebuild), that sacrifice was not the will of God: "I desire mercy and not sacrifice."[19]

Yet the early church, so soon into their birth, reverted back to sacrificial typology, encapsulated in the prayer of rivalry and subsequent scapegoating. What we witness happening in this prayer is mimetic rivalry. The Sanhedrin, who are seeking to stop the preaching and teaching of the early Christian community, are unable to shut up the apostles with their methods of "justice," whereas the early church, led by the dominance of Peter, are *initially* united in condemnation, and execute swift justice upon Ananias and Sapphira, resulting in a fearful obedience.

In each of the "dropping dead" texts that we have mentioned, including Ananias and Sapphira, "justice" is swift. Whether we interpret these texts as indicating actual death, expulsion, or a combination of the two, everything happens very quickly, the problem purged with a great urgency. And that purging happens via *human, not divine*, hands. This is how myths are created.

Whenever you read of a ritual being transgressed and divine judgment falling upon the transgressor, it is an example of a community murder, of scapegoating in action, justified through perceived divine commands. This scapegoating happens in order to maintain the peace of the community in the face of crisis or threat of breakdown of community cohesion. Therefore, with Ananias and Sapphira we have an early example within the new church community of a lynching that will have resulted in either death or expulsion, in order to hold the community together according to the strict boundaries that had already been established.

---

19. Hos 6:6, Matt 9:13 (NKJV).

(De)Stabilized Community

The death/expulsion of Ananias and Sapphira *initially* resolves the crisis, however the unity this act brings—a unity of fear—will dissipate, and the church will find themselves caught up in divisions and disagreements. Whereas in Achan's death the community maintains peace through sacrificial repetition, rituals that remember the first expulsion and ward off further crises, such rituals do not take place after Ananias and Sapphira's scapegoating. This is, then, a "failed" attempt at scapegoating, an attempt to hark back to sacred violence which can never fully succeed again because of the gospel, which has deconstructed it, and which we will come back to. We could then say that the very fact that the scapegoating act fails to produce unity is evidence that the gospel is already at work. Perfect love casts out fear, drawing people together in the Spirit of peace, whereas scapegoating creates a fragile and false unity, its foundations built on fear.

What we do see, rather than a community shaped entirely by the gospel, is the birth of the *ekklesia from the fear that descends* (Acts 5:11). The text then describes the "superfluous" healing miracles that are a consequence of such fear, culminating in the image of Peter's healing shadow: when great fear captures a community, the people will assign great power—even supernatural power—to their leaders, elevating them to divine status. Fear of being expelled or killed will generate an obedience powerful enough to create illusions and myths that follow the leaders wherever they go. Examine the narratives and community dynamics of modern day "health and wealth" televangelists, or the messianic status given to Donald Trump by conspiracy theorists, and you will see how myths and fear generate a following.

Peter is seemingly given a role and status of incredible power. This is seen especially in the description of Peter healing the sick just by his shadow passing over them. In doing this he appears to wield a power not even attributed to Jesus in the Gospels. With nearly all of the healing miracles performed by Jesus, they had a human touch and a personal context. Even when the woman is healed simply by touching the hem of his garment, there is still the human-to-human compassion that flows from within the text. Whereas, here, with Peter, his power seems like that of a "super-apostle," someone with power for power's sake.

In the ancient world the shadow often signified the "spiritual" part of a person. There was a plethora of superstitions connected to the shadow, such as you could cause grave damage to a person by harming their shadow—should such a thing even be possible—with noontime especially dangerous as people were supposedly vulnerable to hexing[20] during this time of the day. Roman philosophers wrote of how someone's shadow could harm you, while ancient Greek historians said that if you entered the temple of Zeus, you'd lose your shadow and die. Peter, then, is presented as being filled up completely with divine healing power, as though this power overflows from within him. Today, we could say this is symbolic of a "theology of glory" rather than the Pauline theology of the cross, where strength is found in weakness.

Martin Luther called the church to be shaped by *theologia crucis*, a theology that recognized that it is through the Crucified Lord that we encounter the fullness of God. In the Heidelberg Disputation that took place on April 26, 1518, Luther said that a person "deserves to be called a theologian . . . who comprehends the visible and manifest things of God seen through suffering and the cross." A theology of glory, according to Luther, "calls evil good and good evil," whereas a theology of the cross "calls the thing what it actually is."

"Therefore," Luther continues about those committed to a *theologia gloriae*, "he prefers works to suffering, glory to the cross, strength to weakness, wisdom to folly, and, in general, good[21] to evil." Luther is unequivocal of what a theology of the cross as

---

20. Perhaps, today, many people would associate hexing with the world of *Harry Potter* and dark magic. Yet its origins date much further back. At the time of Jesus and the disciples, hexing was a form of elaborate curse, with evidence of hexes being used by the ancient Egyptians, Greeks, Romans, and Jews against their enemies, to bring trouble and bad luck.

21. Here, "good" means evil, a good defined by *theologia gloriae* rather than a good defined by *theologia crucis*.

opposed to a theology of glory looks like; only one knows the God who is "hidden in suffering."[22] The young Lutheran, German pastor Dietrich Bonhoeffer (1906–45), who opposed the Nazis during the Second World War, put it like this:

> In a world where success is the measure and justification of all things, the figure of him who was sentenced and crucified remains a stranger.[23]

And, as the second-century Epistle to Diognetus says,

> If you also desire [to possess] this faith, you likewise shall receive first of all the knowledge of the Father. . . . And if you love Him, you will be an imitator of His kindness. . . . For it is not by ruling over his neighbor, or by seeking to hold supremacy over those that are weaker, or by being rich, and showing violence toward those that are inferior . . . can anyone by these things become an imitator of God. . . . On the contrary, He who takes on the burden of his neighbor, . . . he who, whatsoever things he has received from God, by distributing to the needy, becomes a god to those who receive [his benefits]; he is an imitator of God.[24]

Peter operates far differently, in the form of a super-apostle, unable to be an imitator of God, and is hard to distinguish from a pagan wonder-worker like Apollonius of Tyana.[25] Yet God in Christ called his followers to imitate him as one who is not our rival, never withholding, never trying to trap us or trick us, never trying to hold onto power or reveal himself through power,[26] but, rather, a God who is powerless: "God let's himself be pushed out of the world on to the cross. He is weak and powerless in the world."[27]

---

22. Luther, "Heidelberg," paras. 22–24.
23. Bonhoeffer, *Ethics*, 77.
24. Epistle to Diognetus, 10.
25. A traveling wonder-working Greek philosopher who was believed to have lived in the Roman province of Cappadocia during the first century.
26. Phil 2:6–8.
27. Bonhoeffer, *Letters and Papers*, 196.

This God is not full of power, but full of grace, and rich in mercy. As Sam Wells points out,

> We are overwhelmed. God's inexhaustible creation, limitless grace, relentless mercy, enduring purpose, fathomless love: it is too much to contemplate, assimilate, understand. This is the language of abundance . . . a tidal wave of glory.[28]

In contrast to this beautiful picture, the actions of the church against Ananias and Sapphira reveal a community—or, at very least, a leadership—who are ruthless and rivalistic, portraying God as someone who is in competition with our affection and desires. Yet, as is revealed in Christ, God has never been this way, and, from the very beginning, has always made the first move toward us in order to heal and redeem. Christ came to help shift our distorted perceptions of God. Any change in God happens not within the Trinitarian life, but *according to our perception of who this God is*, and it is here that we now turn.

---

28. Wells, *God's Companions*, 7.

5

Genesis and Acts

Boy: Do not try and bend the spoon. That's impossible. Instead only try to realize the truth.

Neo: What truth?

Boy: There is no spoon.

Neo: There is no spoon?

Boy: Then you'll see that it is not the spoon that bends, it is only yourself.

THE MATRIX[1]

COMMENTATORS HAVE NOTICED A link between Exod 3—God's revelation to Moses as unchangeable—and Gen 1. The *Targum Neofiti*, recognizing the connection and world play between these two passages, interprets Exod 3:14 in unfamiliar, almost cryptic language as: "The one who said and the world came into existence from the beginning; and is to say to it again: Be, and it will be, has sent me to you."[2] The appearance of the Hebrew word—translated as "I AM"—three times in the verse (holding to the Hebrew significance of repetition), highlights the threefold difference of

---

1. The Wachowskis, *Matrix*.
2. McNamara, *Targum Neofiti 1*, 19–20.

meaning of the word in its usage; past, present and future. In Gen 1 the writer continually uses a Hebrew word translated as "let there be," which is a play on the name of God; all the letters for this Hebrew word are part of the divine name as revealed to Moses in Exod 3. What does all this mean? In time and space, creation and redemption, history and potential, God doesn't change but is always in a movement of creativity. There is an invitation continually extended toward humanity to be partakers and sharers in that divine creative work.

There was, then, no change in God at the fall. Adam and Eve simply saw God differently because they believed they had become God's rival. What I mean by this is that humanity began in a harmonious relationship with creation and its Creator, "sharers in the divine nature," as the New Testament puts it. Then a change occurs, and humanity see God as a rival, as someone whom they are in competition with, no longer the source of their joy, but one who is *withholding from them*, denying them potentiality so, according to their own perspective, they cannot become an equal with God.[3] Yet God does not change. Hence why it is their *perception* of God that we are witnessing being played out in Gen 3, where myth conceals God behind human jealousy, and the resulting need to create a punitive god. But God has not changed. The prologue to John's Gospel makes it clear that what we see in Christ is that it is *we who expel God*, not the other way around.[4]

Although hidden behind myth within the text at time, the nonviolent, nonrivalrous God is still there in the early chapters

3. There are other ways of reading the Eden narrative which highlight the rivalistic change in humanity toward God. For instance, David Bentley Hart makes the point that when these narratives are *confined to the purely literal level*, without spiritual (that is, allegorical) supplement, "then their message gets lost, and we end up with gods of various powers in a state of panic and rivalry, searching for ways to keep humanity in the dark as to their own capacity and power." See Hart, *Tradition and Apocalypse*, 91–92. Elsewhere I have explored the rivalry beyond the Eden narrative, specifically in regard to Cain and Abel. See Haward, *Be Afraid*, 20.

4. "He was in the cosmos, and through him the cosmos came to be, and the cosmos did not recognize him. He came to those things that were his own, and they who were his own did not accept him." John 1:10–11.

of Genesis, such as the abundance of creation, making clothes for Adam and Eve,[5] and scattering humankind away from Babel.[6] Some of the church fathers, and certain parts of Eastern Orthodox theology, stress that the expulsion of humanity from Eden, and the excluding angel with the fiery sword, are also aspects of God's care for humanity; the prevention of them from eating from the tree of life, and therefore from becoming immortal in sin/separation from God. Irenaeus of Lyon (ca. 120–ca. 200) puts it like this:

> Wherefore also He drove him out of Paradise, and removed him far from the tree of life, not because He envied him the tree of life, as some venture to assert, but because He pitied him, [and did not desire] that he should continue a sinner forever, nor that the sin which surrounded him should be immortal, and evil interminable and irremediable. But He set a bound to his [state of] sin, by interposing death, and thus causing sin to cease, Romans 6:7 putting an end to it by the dissolution of the flesh, which should take place in the earth, so that man, ceasing at length to live to sin, and dying to it, might begin to live to God.[7]

It is possible, then, to regard the early church—in their murder of Ananias and Sapphira—in a similar typology as Adam and Eve;

---

5. In certain mystical traditions, Gen 3:21 is interpreted as the sinlessness and then fall of humanity. Before the fall, humanity shone with brilliance, their light a reflection of the paradise in which they dwelled. Due to sin, their celestial light is replaced by "garments of skin." As a result, the light that once shone was dimmed. Here, then, we can see a significant insight into Christ's message, "I am the light of the cosmos; whoever follows me most surely will not walk in darkness, but rather will possess the light of life." John 8:12.

6. In the *Targum Neofiti*, humanity has become undifferentiated, not only in their desire to build a tower at Babel, but also in their desire to make war: "Let us make ourselves an idol on top of it, and let us put in its hand a sword to make war against him." God's desire to confound their desires can be interpreted not as a punishment, but as a deep concern for their welfare, an attempt to help humanity find their way home, from the east. The *Targum Neofiti* says, "*bns'm mqdm*, 'in their journeying (=when they journeyed) from the East' . . . takes 'journeying' in the moral sense and understands *qdm* (East or Early) as a name for God." *Targum Neofiti*, 84.

7. Irenaeus, *Against Heresies*, 3.23.

those who seek and see a withholding god who operates within an economy of exchange. In other words, a Deuteronomic god who only brings blessing when the prohibitions have been adhered to, and the right sacrifices have been given—as we see in the Achan narrative—or a god who holds back blessing, a god of scarcity who brings shame and punishment when the right sacrifices have not been given.[8] Not only that, but the word *sin* is first used in Scripture when Cain kills Abel; Cain's perception of God is a withholding god, and Abel's blood cries out for vengeance. Peter's condemnation of Ananias and Sapphira carries a similar typology of sin, prohibition, and vengeance.

But we can also see Peter as the one who imitates the punitive and jealous aspects of the god *he perceives*—this withholding and punishing god—rather than the God of forgiveness revealed in Jesus. I understand this is a remarkable and jarring statement, especially when we consider who it is I am making the statement about. Yet we need to recognize that even after all that Peter had experienced and heard from Christ, he chose the path of believing in sacred violence. Perhaps this is why tradition has it that Peter requested to be crucified upside down, a dawning realization that, in the murder of Ananias and Sapphira, he had distorted the message of the cross, operating out of sacred violence, rather than the gospel of peace?

A Falling Church

The early church, like humanity from its beginning, even in the intimate presence of divine love, failed to see the inclusive God of nonviolent embrace. The death of Ananias and Sapphira, and the resulting fear that gripped the believers, could be seen, then, as a

---

8. "See, I am setting before you today a blessing and a curse: the blessing, if you obey the commandments of the Lord your God that I am commanding you today; and the curse, if you do not obey the commandments of the Lord your God but turn from the way that I am commanding you today, to follow other gods that you have not known." Deut 11:26–28 (NRSV).

type of "fall," a distortion of divine perception, a wandering "east"[9] away from recognizing the God of inexhaustible grace.

The full meaning of the gospel, in its universality and inclusion, was something the early church would struggle to comprehend, a struggle that has gripped the church throughout its existence. If you consider today how difficult it for Christians to accept the universal salvation of God, it is no wonder the universality of the gospel at Pentecost, with the promise of the Spirit being poured out upon all people,[10] was interpreted, at times, as a *particular* people. Pentecost was an *anticipation* of the full inclusion of the gentiles into God's kingdom, but this clearly is not initially embraced by the early church. While theological and ideological, this exclusivity was also a cultural mindset, one that does not change overnight; it transforms very slowly. Although we see at the outset of the Gospel of Luke a Jewish-centered expectation, its trajectory is for the inclusion of the gentiles. However, in the first chapter of Acts we have returned again to a faith centered upon an exclusivity of Jewish expectations. Notice how the disciples ask Jesus, just before his ascension, "Lord, are you restoring the kingdom of Israel at this time?" (Acts 1:6). Such a question after the inclusivity of Luke's ending to his Gospel seems strange,[11] but perhaps he is using this as a tool to show the reader how slow the disciples (and humanity) are in understanding the universality of the gospel. How many Christians today truly believe in a universal gospel? How many fall into rival camps of "us" and "them," believing only the elect will be saved, rather than a vision that all are elect in Jesus Christ? But Acts, like church history, reveals a mixed picture.

---

9. Throughout the early chapters of Genesis, wandering east is analogous to moving away from God's presence. The Magi's journey, from the east, is the declaration that, in Christ, all of humanity are now brought back into the presence of God.

10. Acts 2:17.

11. "And he said to them: 'Thus it has been written that the Anointed will suffer and rise again from the dead on the third day, And in his name transformation of the heart and forgiveness of sins will be proclaimed to all the nations, beginning from Jerusalem. You are witnesses of these things.'" Luke 24:46–48.

The early chapters of Acts, to use Girardian terms, are "a text in travail." The church is, on one hand, rivalistic and violent, as we saw earlier with the combative prayer, and the murder of Ananias and Sapphira, seduced, perhaps, by ideas of a messianic age that would be established through bloodshed. Yet there are also moments of universality, an understanding of God's universal embrace found in Christ.

> So change your hearts and turn about, so that your sins may be expunged, So that times of renewal may come from before the face of the Lord, and he may send the Anointed who was appointed for you beforehand, Jesus, Whom heaven must hold until the times of that Restoration [*apokatastaseōs*] of all things of which God spoke through the mouth of his holy prophets an age ago. (Acts 3:19–21)

Universal *apokatastasis*, or "restoration of all things," in later Christian thought, would come to refer not only to the final reconstitution of the cosmos, but also to the final salvation and glorification of all of creation and of every person. Quite simply, certain early Christian thinkers believed God would gather *all humanity*, and *all created things*, in totality, into his reconciling wholeness.

However, despite these eschatological visions of supreme hope, the early community is still acting with exclusivity, with a failure to include gentiles. Even after Peter's vision that led him to the house of Cornelius,[12] these exclusive ideological beliefs remained for him, so much so that Paul had to confront him in front of others as to the separating of himself from the gentile believers in Antioch.[13]

It appears that there are still elements, in the faith of this early community, of a focus upon a violent and exclusive idea of God. Yet, as we shall see, the gospel, found in the life and teachings of Jesus, and proclaimed by Paul, would not be hindered; the Spirit will always find a way through. The stone has been rolled away

---

12. See Acts 10.
13. See Gal 2.

from the tomb, the eighth day of creation is upon us, and God is bringing humanity, who are all his children, home.

Speaking of the tomb, I mentioned earlier the significance of the tomb stone being rolled away before our detour through Acts and Genesis. Let us return, then, to the revelatory nature of the death and resurrection of Jesus.

6

Mercy Not Sacrifice

Cruelty is a gift humanity has given itself.

HANNIBAL LECTER, *HANNIBAL*[1]

MATTHEW'S GOSPEL RECORDS THAT at the crucifixion of Jesus the veil of the sanctuary was rent in two (Matt 27:51). The veil "conceals the mystery of sacrifice,"[2] yet with its tearing from top to bottom God reveals to humanity that the place of sacrifice is *empty* of his very presence; when the curtain was torn apart at the death of Jesus, it revealed that God was not in the sanctuary. This is the *prestige* moment.

> Every great magic trick consists of three parts or acts. The first part is called "The Pledge." The magician shows you something ordinary: a deck of cards, a bird, or a man. He shows you this object. Perhaps he asks you to inspect it to see if it is indeed real, unaltered, normal. But of course, it probably isn't. The second act is called "The Turn." The magician takes the ordinary something and makes it do something extraordinary. Now you're looking for the secret, but you won't find it, because of course

---

1. Navarro, *Hannibal*.
2. Girard, *Things Hidden*, 234.

you're not really looking. You don't really want to know. You want to be fooled. But you wouldn't clap yet. Because making something disappear isn't enough; you have to bring it back. That's why every magic trick has a third act, the hardest part, the part we call "The Prestige."[3]

The revelation that God is not behind the curtain, that God does not command nor desire sacrifice, that God is a God of nonviolence and peace, shatters our perceptions of who God is.[4] Sacrifice is so embedded within our consciousness that when the curtain falls away, we expect a god to be there, a god who demands blood. Yet behind the curtain of sacrifice there is no God, only us: *We are the ones who demand blood to be spilled so that our wrath can be placated.* This is *the prestige*, the finale of the trick where the magician stuns the audience, causing the crowd to puzzle over how such a thing is even possible.[5] For us, God is the magician, revealing, through the death of the Son, that the desire for blood was always human, and the need for sacrifice was always human. And still today we can't believe it, continue to puzzle over it, and deny such a thing could be possible. "Surely," we say to ourselves, "sacrifice has always been God's plan?" No! And the falling curtain has revealed this truth into the very fabric of existence; God desires mercy, not sacrifice. God has always desired mercy, not sacrifice,

---

3. According to John Cutter in *The Prestige*, directed by Christopher Nolan.

4. God has a habit of doing this. My favorite moment in Scripture of God utterly destroying our ideas of what we believe God should be like happens in Rev 5:4–7: "And I was weeping copiously because no one was found worthy to open the book or to look at it. And one of the elders says to me, 'Do not weep; look: The lion of the tribe of Judah, the root of David, has conquered, so as to open the book and its seven seals.' And in the midst of the throne and the four animals, and in the midst of the elders, I saw a suckling lamb standing, like one that had been slaughtered, having seven horns and seven eyes—which are God's seven Spirits sent forth into all the earth—And he came and took it from the right hand of the one sitting on the throne." We are looking for a lion, expecting a lion, sure that only a lion can truly be our mighty, powerful God, yet what we get is a suckling lamb, and not just any lamb, but a slaughtered one! God will always break our expectations of what we think he should be like. The Crucified God reveals the fullness of who God is to us.

5. I have explored the idea of *the prestige* previously, but from a different perspective. See Haward, *Ghost of Perfection*, 86–88.

because this is what God is like. But it is not just the curtain tearing that brings this revelation.

At Jesus's death the earth shakes, splitting rocks, and opening the tombs of "those holy ones."[6] We are then presented with this strange scene:

> And, coming forth from the tombs, they went into the holy city after his resurrection and appeared to many. (Matt 27:53)

Girard believes this moment is the "bringing to light" of all the victims of sacrifice, those who since the foundation of the world have been murdered to maintain the life of the community.[7] Jesus is quoted in Luke declaring to the Pharisees and Teachers of the law,

> Alas for you, because you build the tombs of the prophets, and your fathers killed them. You, therefore, are witnesses that you consent to your father's works, because they killed them and you do the building. Thus also the Wisdom of God said, 'I will send prophets and Apostles to them, and some of them they will kill and persecute,' so that all the blood of the prophets shed since the foundation of the cosmos will be required of this generation, from the blood of Abel to the blood of Zachariah who perished between the altar and the sanctuary; yes, I tell you, it will be required of this generation. (Luke 11:47–51)

Furthermore, quoting Ps 78, Matthew's Gospel applies to Jesus the saying "I shall open my mouth in parables, I shall utter things that have been hidden since the creation."[8] In other words, sacrifice as a tool used by humans to placate their own wrath has been hidden behind sacred violence since the very first murder. Yet now, in and through Jesus, it has been revealed. What has been concealed since the foundation of human communities—scapegoating as the very

---

6. Matt 27:52.
7. See Girard, *Things Hidden*, 234–35.
8. Matt 13:35.

thing that forms human communities—has been brought into the light. The splitting stones at the death of Jesus, and the removal of the tomb stone at his resurrection, exposes the sacrificial mechanism as false. Achan and his family were murdered by stones, the king of Ai was buried beneath stones, and Joshua built an altar of stones to affirm their deaths through the reconstitution of sacrifice; through Jesus, God has exposed these stones as monuments of murder, and as nothing to do with the divine life. The stones of murder have been rolled away, split apart and shattered, exposed for what they truly are. These stones act as a testimony against scapegoating, so much so that they would even cry out if anyone attempted to conceal the myth of sacrifice (Luke 19:40).

Jesus reveals that from Abel, from whose murder the foundation of human communities evolved, to Zechariah, murder has sustained human communities, performed in the power of sacrifice as a means of catharsis for mimetic rivalry and violence. Therefore, it is an act that has been hidden as to its true nature because of its seductive power. Jesus exposes that which has been hidden since the foundation of the world, and through his death and resurrection, by the Spirit, brings to light the scapegoating mechanism, and disarms the power of sacrifice, revealing God's absence from it. As Jesus says, "The Son can do nothing from himself, except what he sees the Father doing; for whatever things the one does, these same things the Son likewise also does."[9] In the death and resurrection of Jesus the stones of sacrifice are removed once and for all.

Achan is killed by the community in order to restore peace and regain divine favor. Yet in the death of Jesus we discover that God desires mercy not murder. The stone removal from the tomb of Jesus is symbolic of all stone altars being removed by God, exposing the scapegoating myth and God's total rejection of sacrifice. Indeed, whereas in the past the community offered their sacrifice to God, God upends this process in Christ, *by offering himself to humanity*. Paul writes,

---

9. John 5:19.

> For all have sinned and fall short of God's glory, being made upright as a gift by his grace, through the manumission fee paid in the Anointed One, Jesus: Whom God set forth as a place of atonement though faith in his blood, as a demonstration of his justice through the dismissal of past sins in God's clemency—for the demonstration of his justice in the present season—that he might be just and show him who is of Jesus' faith to be upright. (Rom 3:23–26)

Here Paul inverts the traditional understanding of sacrifice so that we come to understand that God offers *God's self* to a humanity bound up in the contagion of violence, and disease of sin and death.

> Therefore, just as sin entered into the cosmos through one man, and death through sin, so also death pervaded all humanity, whereupon all sinned. . . . Just as by one transgression unto condemnation for all human beings, so also by one act of righteousness unto rectification of life of all human beings. (Rom 5:12, 18)

The death of Jesus is an act of peace then, abolishing "the Law consisting in commandments in ordinances,"[10] and shattering "the interposing wall of partition—the enmity,"[11] uniting humanity in God. This act of peace comes about not through a human offering to God but the *offering of God to humanity*.

> The Gospel revelation is the definitive formulation of a truth already partially disclosed in the Old Testament. But in order to come to completion, it requires the good news that God himself accepts the role of the victim of the crowd so that he can save us all. This God who becomes a victim is not another mythic god, but the one God, infinitely good, of the Old Testament.[12]

The key to the scapegoating principle is the transference of the community's fear, chaos, and anxieties upon the victim. Achan, like many others before and after him, fulfills this role. Once Achan and

10. Eph 2:15.
11. Eph 2:14.
12. Girard, *I See Satan*, 130.

his family have been murdered, the fear that drove the community dissipates, the wrath of the community now symbolized by the blood that stains the earth. But, in order to maintain this newfound peace, strict rituals must now be observed, reenacting the murder, over and over. This is why Joshua will build an altar and reintroduce sacrifice to the community; sacrifice will be that which now drives the community forward in its fragile sense of unity.

God's acceptance of this sacrificial role, in Christ, is to expose once and for all the divine absence within all acts of "sacred" violence. As John's prologue makes clear, it is we who expel God, not the other way around.[13] Yet the scapegoating myth persists, the belief that it is through the expulsion of others that sin is dealt with, and thus peace restored with God. Achan and his family are the recipients of this myth, and, according to the text, accept it. As we have already noted, this expulsion and exclusivity is seen clearly in the way the Jerusalem church handles Ananias and Sapphira. Over and over again humanity engages in these acts of scapegoating, so certain of their divine mandate, convinced that through the rejection of this person/people, peace will be restored, the crisis averted, and God's blessing will return.

The life and ministry of Jesus, however, not only reframes this concept of restored peace but utterly destroys it; it is God who enters into sinful human condition, and thus redeems it, bringing peace through God's own infusing presence—not through expulsion or separation—taking that which is sinful and offering a redeeming cure through this presence. As Eusebius declares,

> But he alone having reached our deep corruption, he alone having taken upon himself our labors, he alone having suffered the punishments due to our impieties, having recovered us who were not half dead merely, but were already in tombs and sepulchers, and altogether foul and offensive, saves us both anciently and now, by his beneficent zeal, beyond the expectation of any one, even of ourselves, and imparts liberally of the Father's

---

13. "He was in the cosmos . . . and the cosmos did not recognize him. He came to those things that were his own, and they who were his own did not accept him." John 1:10–11.

benefits—he who is the giver of life and light, our great Physician and King and Lord, the Christ of God.[14]

Whereas with the Israelites and Achan, "sin" enters the community through the devoted things being brought into the camp, with the only "cure" offered through expulsion, in Christ, healing is found through God becoming what we are,[15] enabling us to then be "communicants in the divine nature, having escaped from the decay that is in the cosmos on account of desire."[16] In other words, Jesus heals our sin by bringing us into his presence, entering the community and "dragging" to himself all of humanity. He redeems "all things" through presence not expulsion, reconciliation not destruction, bringing peace through the offering of himself. Our desire drives our rivalry, consumed, as we are, by the need to have what our neighbor has. Yet in Christ we find a God who is abundance, a God who does not withhold but gives freely, and invites us to share in that eternal grace.

That God "pitches a tent among us" is not that God becomes the crowd, rather, that the Word takes on the flesh of all humanity, bringing all of humanity into the Trinitarian life. As Paul highlights in the letter to the church in Galatia, all racial, social, economic, religious distinctions have now been replaced, with humanity now defined according to Christ (Gal 3:28). True humanity is revealed by Jesus, determined not by the will of the crowd—notice how, in the Gospels, Jesus always remains outside of the crowd—but by the will of the Father.

> For in no other way could we have learned the things of God, unless our Master, existing as the Word, had become human. For no other being had the power of revealing to us the things of the Father, except His own proper Word.[17]

---

14. Eusebius, *Church History*, 10.4.12.
15. Irenaeus, *Against Heresies*, 5.1.
16. 2 Pet 1:4.
17. Irenaeus, *Against Heresies*, 5.1.

The gospel revelation is that God becomes the victim of the crowd, exposing the violence of the crowd, and the potential for its will to become murderous. This mob's will is opposed to the will of God, whose cruciform revealed will is one of forgiveness. Christian theology continues to maintain that at the cross of Jesus we encounter the fullness of God, or, as Martin Luther states, people deserve "to be called a theologian . . . who comprehend . . . the visible and manifest things of God seen through suffering and the cross."[18]

Violence, then, can be seen as a human problem, not a divine one: "Violence has no place in the character of God,"[19] as the second-century Epistle to Diognetus declares. Or, as Clement of Rome puts it near the end of the first century, "Let us reflect how free from wrath He is towards all His creation."[20] Jesus's life, death, and resurrection "unmasks and thus ends religion based on sacrifice or retributive violence."[21] In the death of Jesus we see the innocent victim get crucified, and we know that this death is unlawful and unjust. In centuries past, the murder of the scapegoat would have been justified in its ability to resolve the crisis of mimetic rivalry. This mythic lie is heard through Caiaphas when he declares, "You do not understand that it is better for you to have one man die for the people than to have the whole nation destroyed."[22] However, in the death of Jesus, his innocence is in full view. The story is no longer told from the viewpoint of the collective, the murderers; rather, it is told from the viewpoint of the innocent victim, the victim being God.

> The Cross is the supreme scandal . . . because . . . it discredits and deconstructs all the gods of violence, since it reveals the true God, who has not the slightest violence in him. Since the time of the Gospels, mankind as a

---

18. Luther, "Heidelberg," para. 23.
19. Epistle to Diognetus, 7.
20. Clement, *First Epistle of Clement*, 19.
21. Weaver, *Nonviolent Atonement*, 51.
22. John 11:50.

whole has always failed to comprehend this mystery, and it does so still.[23]

There is no violence in God, no violence desired from God; the cross is the full absorption of all *our* violence. "In the end, the gospels . . . show that the Love divine must itself suffer in the full most extreme worldly consequences of violence, in order that the lie at the heart of the archaic sacred be ultimately 'nailed.'"[24] In other words, Jesus reveals the lie of the scapegoat mechanism once and for all. Previously the sacrifice of an innocent victim to the gods, although a murderous act, is seen as sacred because it "limits/contains violence, including murder, in everyday life."[25] Žižek continues,

> Therein resides the world-historical rupture introduced by Christianity: now we know [the truth about the sacred], and can no longer pretend that we don't. . . . The impact of this knowledge is not only liberating, but deeply ambiguous: it also deprives society of the stabilizing role of scapegoating and thus opens up the space for violence not contained by any mythic limit.[26]

This is our great challenge: Christianity tells the truth about sacred violence, thus rendering it empty of its seductive and creative force, yet leaving us with a very real dilemma as to how we might respond to violence in a way that does not destroy us. And this is where we turn next.

---

23. Girard, *Things Hidden*, 429–30.
24. Paul Gifford, "Homo Religiosus," 334.
25. Žižek, *God in Pain*, 63–64.
26. Žižek, *God in Pain*, 63–64.

7

The Victim's Story

In our sleep, pain, which we cannot forget, falls drop by drop upon the heart until, in our own despair, against our will, comes wisdom through the awful grace of God.

WILLIAM PETER BLATTY, *THE EXORCIST*[1]

THE UNIQUENESS OF THE Gospels is that we are given the perspective of the victim, each of the Gospel accounts telling the life and story of Jesus as one who dies as the innocent victim. Throughout history, myths are created about victims to cover up their murder by the community. These stories always justify the death of the scapegoat, the murderous guilt of the community rendered innocent, while the victim is declared guilty. Take, for instance, a story written in the third century, supposedly about Apollonius of Tyana, a famous pagan wonder-worker in the first century, and the death of a beggar in the city of Ephesus.

> When the plague began to rage in Ephesus, and no remedy sufficed to check it, they sent a deputation to Apollonius. . . . He . . . called together the Ephesians, and said: "Take courage, for I will today put a stop to the

---

1. Blatty, *Exorcist*, 87.

course of the disease." And with these words he led the population entire to the theatre, where the images of the Averting god had been set up. And there he saw what seemed an old mendicant artfully blinking his eyes as if blind . . . and he was clad in rags and was very squalid of countenance. Apollonius therefore ranged the Ephesians around him and said: "Pick up as many stones as you can and hurl them at this enemy of the gods."

Now the Ephesians wondered what he meant, and were shocked at the idea of murdering a stranger so manifestly miserable; for he was begging and praying them to take mercy upon him. Nevertheless, Apollonius insisted and egged on the Ephesians to launch themselves on him and not let him go. And as soon as some of them began to take shots and hit him with their stones, the beggar who had seemed to blink and be blind, gave them all a sudden glance and showed that his eyes were full of fire. Then the Ephesians recognized that he was a demon, and they stoned him so thoroughly that their stones were heaped into a great cairn around him.

After a little pause Apollonius bade them remove the stones and acquaint themselves with the wild animal which they had slain. When therefore they had exposed the object which they thought they had thrown their missiles at, they found that he had disappeared and instead of him there was a hound who resembled in form and look a Molossian dog, but was in size the equal of the largest lion; there he lay before their eyes, pounded to a pulp by their stones and vomiting foam as mad dogs do.[2]

Begging was commonplace during this time in Ephesus, and beggars would frequently gather at the Ephesian theater. So it is no wonder that Apollonius took the crowd to the theater, for it would be a place certain to have misfits and outcasts wandering around. The so-called wonder-worker identifies a beggar who, he declares, is the cause of the plague ravaging the city, an "enemy of the gods." As we have explored together, the gods were believed to be bringers of blessing and curse, and during a time of plague the community

---

2. Philostratus, *Life of Apollonius*, 363–67.

will believe that such calamity has come upon them because of disobedience to the laws and rituals of the gods. Apollonius tells the crowd he has identified the one who is bringing such a curse upon Ephesus, and they must stone this beggar to death. Initially, however, the crowd are unwilling to do as the preacher commands them. There is a sense, here, that the crowd can see this man is not guilty, that his "miserable" state bears no relevance to any form of guilt. Yet, as is the case with charismatic preachers, and crowds caught within the fear of a crisis, Apollonius convinces the crowd to "launch themselves on him," and, as soon as the first stone is thrown, the beggar's fate is sealed. The first stone will always lead to the second as the crowd imitates one another, caught up in the power of collective rage.

Notice how the scapegoating myth transforms the beggar into a demon whose death is now fully justified. This is how the murder of innocent victims get covered up, as layer upon layer of myth is transposed onto the story, narrated by those in power, hiding the guilt of the perpetrators behind a veil of sacred violence. That is why the death and resurrection of Jesus is key, for not only do we uncover the scapegoating myth, we also find the God of history.

Finding God

The response of Thomas at the natural end to the Gospel according to John, is one of unambiguous declaration that Jesus is *ho theos*, God in the absolute sense (John 20:28). It is this God, the Son, who was crucified as the innocent victim, who has been raised to life by the Spirit, and vindicated by the God whom he revealed and declared, both in life and death. That Jesus has shown us the innocence of the victim, and that the Gospel tells the story *from the victim's perspective*, means that we now have all that is necessary to refuse the power of the scapegoating myth. To hear the voice of the victim is as needed today as it has always been, which is why *how* we interpret Scripture matters. As Christian communities the church is shaped by its reading of Scripture; theology and ethics cannot be separated. The way such theology and ethics plays out in the real world is vital to the kingdom work the church has been called toward.

For instance, the late black liberation theologian James Cone (1938–2018) once asked the question, "What has the gospel of Jesus Christ to do with the black struggle for justice in the United States?"[3] Cone was seeking to find a way of grounding the identity, character, struggle, and human dignity of black Americans in the person and work of Jesus Christ. As Cone rightly understood it, Jesus sought to "announce good tidings to the destitute, he has sent me out to proclaim release to captives and sight to the blind, to send the downtrodden forth in liberty."[4] Witnessing and experiencing oppression himself, seeing victims of racism all around him, Cone's theology/ethics drove his ethics/theology, grounded within the black experience. To hear the voice of the victim, and call out the sin of the oppressors, shaped the theology of Cone, and rightly so. His lament over moderate white Christians echoed his entire theological project.

> Christ dies not to "save" them but to destroy them so as to recreate them, to dissolve their whiteness in the fire of judgment, for it is only through the destruction of whiteness that the wholeness of humanity may be realized.[5]

Privilege and power have no place within the kingdom of Christ. The Spirit is transforming us into servants, a people who see injustice, who call out the perpetrators of oppression—without becoming oppressors ourselves—and hear the voice of the victims. Cone recognizes "whiteness" not as the color of your skin, but the racist structures that kill and destroy black and brown lives.

> Being black in America has very little to do with skin color. To be black means that your heart, your soul, your mind, and your body are where the dispossessed are. We all know that racist structures will reject and threaten a black man in white skin as quickly as a black man in

---

3. Cone, *Black Theology of Liberation*, xv.
4. Luke 4:18.
5. Cone, *Black Theology of Liberation*, 142.

black skin. It accepts and rewards whites in black skins nearly as well as whites in white skins.[6]

The gospel demands we pay attention to the voice of the victim. Reflecting upon the stories of Achan, Ananias, Sapphira, and beggars in ancient Ephesus has a danger of creating within us a distance to the victim's story, a sense that scapegoating, while an interesting intellectual exercise, has little to do with our modern culture, nor relates in any way to my own life, experience, and ethics. By highlighting Cone's work, we are reminded that in hearing the voice of ancient victims, we are being called to *tune in to the voice of every victim*, and live accordingly.

> Blacks and whites are bound together in Christ by their brutal and beautiful encounter in this land. . . . Whites may be bad brothers and sisters, murderers of their own black kin, but they are still our sisters and brothers. . . . We were made brothers and sisters by the blood of the lynching tree, the blood of sexual union, and the blood of the cross of Jesus. . . . If America has the courage to confront the great sin and ongoing legacy of white supremacy with repentance and reparation there is hope.[7]

As I write this governments across the Western world are passing laws, and creating narratives, that will criminalize and scapegoat those people seeking asylum, locking them up in detention camps, deporting them, or doing little to create safe routes for them to enter safety. These racist anti-immigration policies, driven by right-wing media, are scapegoating desperate people because of the crises that exist across Western democracies at the moment. Nations are in political turmoil, with capitalism, consumerism, and neoliberalism unable to answer the problems that exist— problems that will grow from the climate crisis. It is a landscape that continues to lurch far right, with a stalling economy, wars and genocide, growing poverty, political corruption, a failing health system, COVID, Brexit, and the radical decline of living standards.

---

6. Cone, *Black Theology and Black Power*, 151.
7. Cone, *Cross and the Lynching Tree*, 166.

The Victim's Story

As such, scapegoats are sought, a people to blame for the problems the country faces. Ever since at least 2012, in my own country, the UK Conservative Party has been victimizing asylum seekers and immigrants. Racist propaganda exploded around the time of the EU Referendum campaign in 2016, with Brexit driving anti-immigration ideology across all sections of UK society.[8] There are victims crying out, and we need to hear them.

The victim's voice is a significant issue within our modern context. The UK grime artist Dave, in his UK number one hit "Black," highlights the reality of how the voice of the oppressed can be distorted as it is narrated *by the oppressor*. He laments the discrimination black people continue to face in Western society. The song makes reference to the slave trade, the assimilation of black culture by white powers, and the depth of suffering infused within black history, a suffering that continues in our current world.[9]

To hear the voice of the victim, whether it is in the Scriptures, within history, or in our society and communities, is to engage and interpret all things christologically. Jesus hears the cry of every victim, and so the church must work as facilitators of justice, listening well to these cries, and imitating Christ within our communities. But to be able to *hear* requires a transition on how we *read*. The Word became flesh, not text, therefore our theology needs to be grounded within the reality of the human condition. It is not enough to say, "I hear you," and then do nothing to combat the oppression victims are under. To be shaped as a people "of the cross" is to walk with victims, to refuse the way of violence and vengeance, to challenge oppression at every turn, and to model forgiveness as the only power capable of transforming the world.

How we read Scripture needs to be transformed. Finding God within the text is vital in enabling the church to resist becoming oppressors. Hearing the voice of Jesus throughout Scripture—the voice of peace and nonviolence—is about exposing the scapegoat myth, reinterpreting every passage of "sacred violence," and

---

8. For more on my analysis of racism, scapegoating, and right-wing politics, see Haward, *Be Afraid*, 44–53.

9. See Dave, "Black."

recognizing that the Trinitarian life has always been self-giving, forgiving, abundant, nonviolent, love.

> The grace and the truth came through Jesus the Anointed. (John 1:18)

The same God who is with us is the God who forsakes us. . . . The same God who makes us to live in the world without the working hypothesis of God is the God before whom we stand continually. Before God, and with God, we live without God. God consents to be pushed out of the world and onto the cross; God is weak and powerless in the world and in precisely this way, and only so, is at our side and helps us. . . . Christ helps us, not by virtue of his omnipotence but rather by virtue of his weakness and suffering! This is the crucial distinction between Christianity and all religions. Human religiosity directs people in need to the power of God in the world, God as deus ex machina. The Bible directs people toward the powerless and suffering of God; only the suffering God can help. To this extent, one may say that the previously described development toward the world's coming of age, which has cleared the way by eliminating a false notion of God, frees us to see the God of the Bible, who gains ground and power in the world by being powerless.

Dietrich Bonhoeffer, *Letters and Papers from Prison*[1]

---

1. Bonhoeffer, *Letters and Papers*, 196–97.

Conclusion

Interpreting Scripture from the perspective of the forgiving victim enables us to come to the story of Achan, Ananias and Sapphira, and Scripture as a whole, and read the "divine" violence within it from another perspective. Because of the gospel and the revelation of Jesus of Nazareth as the forgiving victim, we discover that God exposes the cycle of human violence and thus judges scapegoating as "satanic." Now, it is important to unpack what is meant by the word *satanic*.

Gregory of Nyssa repeatedly said, throughout his writings, that evil was "nonbeing," something that could not exist outside of itself. His brother Basil pursued similar ideas, describing evil as something that does not live but exists as a result of falling away from God. In other words, it is an unreality, something that is not real in the same sense as we say God is real. What we have discovered throughout this book is that violence is a human problem, not a divine one, an evil that leads to destruction, nonbeing. When God is "all in all," evil will have nowhere to "attach" itself, and will dissipate into its reality of nonexistence. Now, that does not mean evil does not have an impact upon the world—of course it does, and we all witness it throughout our lives. But what it does mean is that evil will never share in the triune embrace, when "all will be well," as Julian of Norwich so beautifully attests.

The word *satanic* is a way of describing evil, but who or what is "the satan"? The satan is the accusatory principle, the way we accuse and blame others for the crisis we perceive happening within our lives or community. Every time we point a finger to blame someone else for the crisis around us—such as when Germany pointed the finger at the Jewish community in the 1930s, or how successive Western governments are currently pointing the finger at asylum seekers—we play the part of the satan. There is more to the satanic principle than this, such as deception and death, but it all begins here. Whenever people come together to blame and accuse someone else for their troubles, they are acting satanic. Now, that is not to say we never pursue justice for victims, but that we do not become a mob seeking to scapegoat our way to peace.

The satan, then, is not a fallen angel but a way of being, the power of accusation. Michael Hardin puts it like this:

> Genesis 3 and 4 recount the beginnings of the descent of humanity into a world dominated by sin, violence, and idolatry. Rather than trace the fall of Adam to the breaking of a covenant (which is not mentioned in the text) or to pride (which is not mentioned in the text), or to sex, which occurs after the problem in the garden, we can see the "fall" as the human descent into violence, sacrifice, and culture. What then might the serpent represent? The serpent perfectly represents the mechanism of object mediated desire. . . . It is all about imitated desire and its consequences. . . .
>
> . . . The devil is an anthropological category not a theological one. The devil is about us humans, our violence, our projection, our victimizing, our idolatry. It is not about some supra temporal being that God created. No, we humans created the satan. . . . The satan dwells within us, creates our communities, rules our ideologies. . . . The satanic requires sacrifice. Human sacrifice.[1]

So in essence, we are asking, what is the satan and the nature of the satanic? Moving away from a "personal devil," we discover that the satan is not a person, nor a being created by God, but, rather, *an accusatory principle, originating within human communities, used as way of structuring those communities, based upon the use of violence and scapegoating*; the devil is a "murderer." This point is absolutely key and foundational to our theology, because, if the

---

1. Hardin, "Satan," 22–23.

Conclusion

satan is a murderer, then *God cannot be*. God is nonviolent, self-giving love, and the gospel reveals that God has always been this way. In Christ we discover a God who offers peace, thus showing us that the way of God has never been violent.

"I AM WHO I AM."[2]

"Jesus said to them, 'Amen, amen, I tell you, before Abraham came to be, I AM.'"[3]

The unchanging God comes to us in Christ and refuses the way of sacrifice, violence, or retribution: "I desire mercy not sacrifice."[4]

Reading Scripture according to the "victim of myth"—the community creating stories around the guilt of the scapegoat—means that the death of Achan has been wrongly justified, appealing to notions of God's justice, holiness, and Scripture's inerrancy. For instance, Douglas Earl states,

> Achan, and his story . . . is only a model to follow for behavior in as far as it encourages obedience to the covenant and praise of YHWH and the construction of identity in this way; it is not about the execution of innocent children, a narrative device that serves essentially structural requirements relating to the construction of Israel's identity.[5]

It is remarkable how we are continually able to justify slaughter within the biblical text (and within the world today) by appealing to notions of "obedience," and "identity," and so maintaining the myth of sacred violence. To read Scripture in this way creates a god whose image is no better than the worst of humanity. Saint Isaac the Syrian (ca. 613–ca. 700) believed that such a hermeneutical approach was nothing less than theological "madness."

> That we should imagine that anger, wrath, jealousy, or such like have anything to do with the divine Nature is

---

2. Exod 3:14 (NRSV).
3. John 8:58.
4. Matt 9:13.
5. Earl, "Reading Joshua," 141.

> something utterly abhorrent for us: no one in their right mind, no one who has any understanding (at all) can possibly come to such madness as to think anything of the sort about God. Nor again can we possibly say that He acts thus out of retribution, even though the Scriptures may on the outer surface posit this. Even to think this of God and to suppose that retribution for evil acts is to be found with Him is abominable. . . . Just because (the terms) wrath, anger, hatred, and the rest are used of the Creator, we should not imagine that He (actually) does anything in anger or hatred or zeal. Many figurative terms are employed in the Scriptures of God, terms which are far removed from His (true) nature.[6]

Isaac recognizes the tension that obviously exists between the text and the flesh, between the written word and the Word of God, but refuses to resort to textual literalism. To assign to God any kind of violence within God's own character and nature is "abhorrent," "madness," and "abominable." Now, some might find Isaac's language here uncharitable, intolerant, and at odds with great swaths of thinkers throughout church history—so many have assigned to God's character and nature, through literalist readings of the text, the very things Isaac is dismissing. Yet, in reality, many of the greatest minds in the church, certainly during the first six centuries of its existence, approached Scripture *allegorically*, seeking the spiritual truth according to how Christ is *being revealed* within the text.

Origen of Alexandria (ca. 185–ca. 253) repeatedly said throughout his writings that we may not attribute to God that which is unworthy of God, or unworthy of how God has been revealed in and through Jesus of Nazareth. For Origen, Scripture was that which "represents for us the mysteries of Jesus my Lord."[7] Indeed, for Origen, a spiritual reading of Scripture was the highest goal, a belief that the letter kills, but the Spirit brings life.[8] Origen believed that a literal or historic reading of certain places within

---

6. Isaac of Ninevah, *Second Part*, 2.39.2–3.
7. Origen, *Homilies*, 1.3.
8. Origen, *Homilies*, 9.

CONCLUSION

Scripture was to bring confusion and contradiction, a reading that makes no sense of what the text is describing.

> Do you think the Scripture would contain things contrary to itself? This must not be lightly regarded. Let us return to the spiritual understanding, and you will find that there is nothing conflicting in it.[9]

Origen held that a spiritual reading was the higher reading of Scripture, especially when it came to the texts of violence. So the book of Joshua, for Origen, needed a better interpretation.

> Unless those physical wars bore the figure of spiritual wars, I do not think the books of Jewish history would ever have been handed down by the apostles to the disciples of Christ, who came to teach peace, so that they could be read in the churches.[10]

Both Isaac and Origen understood the theological ramifications of a violent God, and how such a God was utterly in contradiction to the God revealed in Christ. For both these great thinkers of the church the highest goal of Scripture is to hear the voice of Christ from within it, a voice that refuses all violence and calls peace upon all humankind.

Such hermeneutical approaches have been lost at various times throughout the last millennium of the church, kept alive by dissenting voices who understood that there is no dark side to God. But Scripture has too easily been read in such a way as to *continue the cycle of violence through retribution or oppressive acts.* In other words, the voice of the victim has either been lost or used vengefully to justify an ethic of retributive justice that demands God violently "right the wrongs" of the past and present, violently punishing the "enemies" of the church. The Crusades and witch hunts are obvious examples, but so too white Christians in the American South or apartheid South Africa, German Christians in 1930s Germany, and evangelical Christians in Trump's America.

---

9. Origen, *Homilies*, 16.3.
10. Origen, *Homilies*, 15.1.

Not only that, but we can read Scripture to "other" others, believing God is on our side, and against our enemies. Like the rivalistic prayer of the early church in Acts 5, we believe "justice" involves a time when "we" will watch as "they" are punished by God; "we" will feast while "they" will watch;[11] "we" will rejoice while "they" will weep; "we" will be saved while "they" will be condemned. But to read the Bible this way is to listen to the blood of Abel crying out from the ground, calling for retribution; the blood of Jesus speaks something better than that of Abel: forgiveness (Heb 12:24). History continues to teach us that the cycle of violence is unending and destructive.

> The ultimate weakness of violence is that it is a descending spiral, begetting the very thing it seeks to destroy. Instead of diminishing evil, it multiplies it. Through violence you may murder the liar, but you cannot murder the lie, nor establish the truth. Through violence you may murder the hater, but you do not murder hate. In fact, violence merely increases hate. So, it goes. Returning violence for violence multiplies violence, adding deeper darkness to a night already devoid of stars.[12]

To read the Bible from the perspective of the forgiving victim enables us to hear the voice of God from within the text, the voice of peace, compassion, and forgiveness that echoes out into the darkest recesses of our violent ways, refusing the will of the thunderous shouts of the crowd demanding blood, and ushering in the way of love, the way of forgiveness, the way of grace.

---

11. In Ps 23, the psalmist declares that God will "prepare a table before me in the presence of my enemies." Within a retributive justice hermeneutic, here we have God transforming the lot of the oppressed, providing a feast and freedom that the oppressors and enemies of God can only look upon in envy and despair: God has flipped the tables so that his followers can now enjoy the abundance of his favor, while his enemies are left ashamed and in a state of scarcity. However, there is another way to read the text: "You prepare a table before me in the presence of my enemies, and we feast together, reconciled by your divine love." The blood of Jesus reconciles and brings peace (Col 1:20), enemies transformed into brothers and sisters, joined together by the Spirit, "communicants in the divine nature." 2 Pet 1:4.

12. King, *Where Do We Go*, 65–66.

Conclusion

"Daddy, why did God kill all those children?"

In the revelation of Christ, we see that God is nonviolent. Indeed, we see that God has always been nonviolent. *We* create myths to justify our violence, and place upon a victim divine approval of catastrophic events. There is always a narrative *we* can create to assuage the guilt of our inaction, or stories that ensure the gods of history are on our side, stories that dehumanize our enemies. As I have already highlighted, notice how, around the world, lies are currently being created about people seeking asylum, or the dehumanization of children caught in war zones of those who Western governments regard as our enemies. It is quite easy to see the death of the children of our enemy as a sign of God's direct involvement, especially when we believe God is exclusively on our side. But God has no enemies. God is love, and that love breaks out across the whole cosmos, infusing all things with healing and hope, meeting with every person, whether we perceive it or not. God has no place in our desire for the destruction of our enemies. When meaningless[13] suffering and catastrophe falls,[14] like plagues and death, God is not found in the disease, nor the destruction, but in the wails and suffering of those who die and mourn.

God did not kill all those children. God is not violent, and has always been like Jesus. Indeed, God will bring every one of his children—the entirety of humanity—home.

---

13. I use the word *meaningless* here to highlight that suffering has no "higher purpose." Suffering is not part of God's "tapestry" to bring everything together for good, rather, it is cruel and without meaning. Now, that is not to say that God cannot use suffering for our good, but it is to say that God does not inflict suffering for his purposes; such a god would be nothing more than the devil.

14. See appendix 3 below.

Appendix I

Judas Iscariot

For, however many God's promises may be, in him there is the "Yes."
2 Cor 5:19b

WHEN EXPLORING "SACRED VIOLENCE" within the biblical text, the figure of Judas Iscariot is important to discuss. The hermeneutical lens through which we explore his story is vital in avoiding the perpetuation of scapegoating ideology. The story of Judas does not fit the typical scapegoating archetype, yet there are similarities that make it a story worth examining.

Within history there is a general consensus that, in death, Judas was condemned to an eternity of damnation, the ultimate betrayer, unredeemable, accursed for all time. Take, for instance, *Inferno*, the fourteenth-century poem by Dante Alighieri (1265–1321).

Dante is led by Virgil into the ninth circle of hell where they encounter "Dis,"[1] the "Emperor of the sorrowful realm,"[2] who is also known as Satan. Dante describes Satan as having "three faces in his head,"[3] a heretical inversion of the Christian Trinity, a picture

---

1. Dante, *Dante's Inferno*, canto 34, st. 20.
2. Dante, *Dante's Inferno*, canto 34, st. 27–28.
3. Dante, *Dante's Inferno*, canto 34, st. 37.

Appendix I

invoking mockery toward the God worshiped by creation. From each one of these terrible mouths, tears and blood drip down as Satan tortures three different people by holding them in his three mouths, devouring them with his fangs, and flaying them with his claws. Virgil tells Dante to look up at the head of Satan, and study the face in the middle where the greatest pain is being inflicted.

> "That wretch up there whom keenest pangs divide
> Is Judas called Iscariot," said my lord,
> "His head within, his jerking legs outside."[4]

Here in the ninth circle of hell the worst of sinners reside, a place of fear, misery, and utter ruin. It is of no surprise that Dante locates Judas within this place, a place reserved for traitors and betrayers, or the "son of perdition," (John 17:12) as the New Testament puts it. His eternal destruction in hell is described by Dante in the most horrific of ways, but fleetingly, and almost as a passing comment. What is interesting is that Dante locates Judas in the ninth circle rather than the seventh circle where the Wood of the Suicides is located. These woods are where

> No green leaves in that forest, only black;
> no branches straight and smooth, but knotted, gnarled;
> no fruits were there, but briers bearing poison.[5]

Every "knotted" and "gnarled" tree within the wood is a soul trapped, bound within a new existence of misery for eternity.

A bronze plate from the doors of the Benevento Cathedral in Italy illustrates Judas, at his death, being held by Harpies, a winged creature from Greek mythology that were the spirits of sudden, strong gusts of wind that snatched people away, sometimes a creature that was associated with the underworld. Within Dante's world, Harpies were "wide-winged," "lady-faced," with "claws of steel." These Harpies dwell in the seventh circle of hell, in the second ring where the Wood of the Suicides is found. Harpies sit on the branches of the trees where the souls of the damned are now

---

4. Dante, *Dante's Inferno*, canto 34, st. 61.
5. Dante, *Dante's Inferno*, canto 13, st. 4.

entombed. When Dante snaps off a branch, the tree cries out in pain, with blood that flows from the broken branch. "Why does thou rend my bones?"[6] the tree cries out.

He goes on,

> We that are turned to trees were human once;
> Nay, thou shouldest tender a more pious hand
> Though we had been the souls of scorpions.[7]

The Harpies sit on the branches, feeding on the leaves and biting the branches, providing agony to the souls of the suicides. It is little surprise, then, that the picture of the hanged Judas at Benevento Cathedral has Harpies ready to carry him away. Yet, within Dante's world, the seventh circle is not torture enough for the one who betrayed the Son of God. The actions of Judas leave him bound to the very depths of hell, gripped within the mouth of the first betrayer, Satan.

Suicide alone, often believed within much of Christian history, is enough to condemn your soul to hell. Thomas Aquinas (1225–1274), for instance, said that suicide was sinful, a violation to God's order. But language about the condemnation of Judas always seems to be even more severe. The theologian Karl Barth (1886–1968) commenting on the death of Judas, said,

> Judas perished from within himself. . . . His creaturely being could no longer endure the monstrousness of the contradiction in which he had enmeshed himself, and so it had to explode like a released hand-grenade.[8]

Throughout history, across art and literature, the punishment and fate of Judas is unambiguous in its tragedy. And there is little in the New Testament to suggest otherwise.

---

6. Dante, *Dante's Inferno*, canto 13, st. 31.
7. Dante, *Dante's Inferno*, canto 13, st. 37.
8. Barth, *Church Dogmatics* 2/2:470.

Appendix I

The New Testament

The New Testament describes Judas as one whom the devil entered, a thief, traitor, son of perdition, and betrayer. Therefore, we are left with the picture of a man who is utterly appalling, someone for whom we should feel no sympathy, someone who is rotten to the core. Karl Barth says,

> And no matter how we look at it, we cannot say that the universal expressions of horror with which the New Testament surrounds [Judas] are inappropriate. . . . Judas is indeed the "son of perdition," the man into whom the Satan has entered, himself a devil. The New Testament, then, can only reject his repentance, however sincerely he may undertake it.[9]

To read of Judas in the New Testament is to be left with an image of a person who should be utterly scorned and rejected, one whose very life was destined for destruction, whose fate was utter ruin. In the book of Matthew, the death of Judas is recorded like this:

> Then Judas, the one who betrayed him, seeing that he had been condemned, changed his heart and returned the thirty silver pieces to the chief priests and elders, Saying, "I sinned by betraying innocent blood." But they said, "What is it to us? You will see to it." And flinging the silver pieces into the sanctuary he withdrew, and going away he hanged himself. (Matt 27:3–5)

Here we witness the figure of a man swinging and spinning from a tree by his neck, swinging with his bowels hanging out, those bowels swaying below him in a shorter, quicker arc, a symbol and picture of what the New Testament, and later art, wants to leave with us when we think of Judas.

While it might be reasonable to think that Peter, who himself engaged in an act of betrayal, would be sympathetic toward Judas, the book of Acts puts these words in Peter's mouth:

---

9. Barth, *Church Dogmatics* 2/2:471.

> Men, brothers, it was necessary that the scripture be fulfilled, which the Spirit, the Holy one, spoke beforehand through the mouth of David concerning Judas, who became a guide for those who arrested Jesus—For he was numbered among us, and had a share in this ministry—So that from the reward for his injustice this man purchased a field and, having fallen prone in the middle of it, he burst apart and all his entrails were poured out. (Acts 1:16–18)

Karl Barth notes that Judas is described in the New Testament as "one of the twelve," and, therefore, his life was as one of the elected, one of those who walked in intimacy with Jesus during his earthly life. He says,

> His election excels and outshines and controls and directs his rejection: not just partly, but wholly: not just relatively, but absolutely. And this is not because it was not really a serious rejection. It is just because it was so serious. It is just because in this figure if in any biblical figure one perceives nothing at all except divine rejection. This very man, who is wholly rejected, is elect.[10]

He goes on to say, when summing up about the fate of the rejected (as he puts it), that God's desire is that the gospel is preached to the rejected and non-elect, that the rejected are not determined by God to remain rejected, but that they are summoned to faith, and that, on the basis of the election of Jesus, they are summoned to believe in their election.[11] Yet for Judas, according to the New Testament and much of church history, such election will never be possible. Indeed, to make the point with ever greater force, we are told, in Matthew's Gospel, about the prophetic significance of the Field of Blood, which was so named because it was bought with the thirty pieces of silver that Judas used to betray Jesus.

> Then was fulfilled what had been spoken by the prophet Jeremiah when he said, "And I took the thirty silver

---

10. Barth, *Church Dogmatics* 2/2:504.
11. See Barth, *Church Dogmatics* 2/2:506.

pieces, the price of the one on whom a price had been set." (Matt 27:9)

However—and it is here we will begin to unshackle Judas from the chains of condemnation—this is not a quote from Jeremiah at all; it may be a vague reference to Zech 11:13,[12] but the writer of Matthew is being more than adventurous with their application of Scripture. In other words, the desire to condemn Judas exceeds truthful application of the Hebrew Scriptures. The Gospel of Matthew wants to attach the actions of Judas to a fulfillment of Scripture, yet in reality it is not a fulfillment of Scripture at all.

Redeeming Judas

The earliest known depiction of Christ's crucifixion in narrative form is from a small ivory carving, dated in the early part of the fifth century, with Judas hanging from a tree, his face upturned to the branch that suspends him, a bag of silver pieces at his feet.

The character Dr. Hannibal Lecter, in *Hannibal*, the novel by Thomas Harris, delivers a lecture to the Studiolo of the Belle Arti Committee in Florence on the subject of Dante's *Inferno* and Judas Iscariot. In it he makes a link between avarice, treachery, and self-destruction. He says,

> Avarice and hanging are linked in the ancient and medi-aeval mind: St. Jerome writes that Judas' very surname, Iscariot, means "money" or "price," while Father Origen says Iscariot is derived from the Hebrew "from suffocation" and that his name means "Judas the Suffocated."[13]

Judas is a man suffocated by his actions, overwhelmed by the reality that he now faces. As we can see, within the New Testament, history, the arts, within modern parables, Judas is the very figure of self-destruction, not only the betrayer but one who is a warning

---

12. "Then the Lord said to me, 'Throw it into the treasury'—this lordly price at which I was valued by them. So I took the thirty shekels of silver and threw them into the treasury in the house of the Lord."

13. Harris, *Hannibal*, 935.

to us all of how perilous the road of greed really is. Yet not everyone believes Judas is a figure of utter humiliation.

Origen (ca. 184–ca. 253) has a different perspective about the man Judas Iscariot, saying that before the soul of Judas was injured by greed and betrayal, it was "quasi a vineyard in blossom."[14] Origen is very sympathetic toward Judas, and sees in his death an act of repentance.

> The declaration, "I have sinned, in that I have betrayed innocent blood," was a public acknowledgement of his crime. Observe, also, how exceedingly passionate was the sorrow for his sins that proceeded from his repentance, and which would not suffer him any longer to live; and how, after he had cast the money down in the temple, he withdrew, and went away and hanged himself; for he passed sentence upon himself, showing what a power the teaching of Jesus had over this sinner Judas.[15]

It is my belief, in light of all that we have explored through Girardian scapegoat theory, and listening intently to Origen's words, that the picture we have of Judas need not be one of destruction and misery, but that another story can be told, a story that can provide insight and hope. Think upon those six small words in Matthew's Gospel, "Judas had a change of heart"[16] . . .

Hope

The New Testament makes it abundantly clear that death is not the end.

> "Death has been swallowed up in victory. Where, death, is your victory? Where, death, is your sting?" Now death's sting is sin, and sin's power is the Law; But thanks to God who gives us victory through our Lord Jesus the Anointed. (1 Cor 15:51–57)

---

14. Origen, *Song of Songs*, cant. 4.
15. Origen, *Against Celsus*, 2.11.
16. Matt 27:3.

Appendix I

Beyond this life we hope for the life to come, the coming of a time when, as Paul says, "God may be all in all,"[17] a time when, again as Paul says, "All will be given life."[18] Or, as Paul puts it in Romans,

> For if, by the one's transgression, death reigned through the one, so much more will those receiving grace's abundance and the gift of righteousness reign in life through the one Jesus the Anointed—So, then, just as by one transgression unto condemnation for all human beings, so also by one act of righteousness unto rectification of life for all human beings. (Rom 5:17–18)

Our acts of destruction against ourselves, our own wrath and tragedy that manifests itself in various ways throughout human history, is not the final word spoken over us, rather, the Word made flesh speaks "Yes!" and "Amen!" over us.

> For the Son of God, Jesus the Anointed . . . did not become a "Yes" and also a "No"; rather, in him came "Yes." For, however many God's promises may be, in him there is the "Yes"; therefore, through him there is also our "Amen" to God. (2 Cor 5:19–20)

Suicide, then, is not the final word spoken over Judas, and it is not the final word spoken over all who have taken their own lives. Jesus is supreme. Jesus is King. Jesus is Lord: he is the Word who has the final word over all humanity.

Judas had a change of heart and repented of his actions. His death by suicide was an expression of his repentance, an expression of extreme remorse, overwhelmed by sorrow, a sentence he passed upon himself, trusting himself, in the only way he knew how, into the care of God. Judas is seeking redemption. All that we have discovered about God in these pages reveals that, in the spirit of George MacDonald, God is for us; even when he must be against us, he is for us.

While the early Christians condemned Judas as guilty, his death does not act as a means of catharsis for the community, nor

---

17. 1 Cor 15:28.
18. 1 Cor 1:22.

does it bring peace. His death certainly serves as a warning, much like Achan's, yet there is little in the text to suggest that he was a scapegoat in the same way. But, just as Achan was condemned to judgment and destruction by the community, so too Judas is regarded as abandoned by God. The similarities echo out across time and space. But, as with Achan, the story that surrounds Judas is not the final word that needs to be spoken over him: God will not abandon him, just as he will never abandon us.

The movement of God is always toward humanity, an inexhaustible well of grace and forgiveness, the longing to bring every person into the divine embrace.[19] Indeed, Paul consistently teaches that in Christ *every person will be saved*. I wonder why the church has not always emphasized verses like the following:

> For just as in Adam all die, so also in the Anointed [Christ] all will be given life. (1 Cor 15:22)

> For the grace of God has appeared, giving salvation to all human beings. (Titus 2:11)

This universality is seen across Paul's writings.

> So, then, just as through one transgression came condemnation for all human beings, so also through one act of righteousness came a rectification of life for all human beings; for just as by the heedlessness of the one man the many were rendered sinners, so also by the obedience of the one the many will be rendered righteous. (Rom 5:18–19)

It is a vision of Christ's lordship and victory that all have been drawn into.

> For which reason God also exalted him on high and graced him with the name that is above every name, so that at the name of Jesus every knee should bend—of beings heavenly and earthly and subterranean—and every tongue gladly confess that Jesus the Anointed is Lord, for the glory of God the Father. (Phil 2:9)

---

19. 2 Pet 3:9.

Appendix I

> For in him all the Fullness was pleased to take up a dwelling, and through him to reconcile all things to him, making peace by the blood of his cross [through him], whether the things on the earth or the things in the heavens. (Col 1:19–20)

> For God shut up everyone in obstinacy so that he might show mercy to everyone. (Rom 11:32)

And then we have examples in the Gospels like these:

> And I, when I am lifted up from the earth, will drag everyone to me. (John 12:32)

> Until John, there were the Law and the prophets; since then the good tidings of God's Kingdom are being proclaimed, and everyone is being forced into it. (Luke 16:16)

The point I am making is that Judas, like every person, is not excluded from the relational presence of God, no matter how far someone has traveled "east." We see in Christ that God is not a withholding God, nor is God a rival, nor a vampiric deity that demands blood. Rather, God is Love, and in him there is no fear, no darkness at all. It is this love that we are called to imitate, this life that we should desire in order to bring peace. Truly unconditional love, given by the Spirit, recognizes that only when every human is redeemed within the embrace of God can every person be truly free: perfect love casts out fear. For heaven to be truly bliss, every person *has* to be saved. Unconditional love, as revealed by Jesus, means that even one lost soul—whoever that soul was—would wound those in bliss with such force because every person will be filled with the same love of Christ; heaven would be filled with nothing but tears, and thus could no longer be bliss. George MacDonald (1824–1905) beautifully describes it thus:

> Who, that loves his brother, would not, upheld by the love of Christ, and with a dim hope that in the far-off time there might be some help for him, arise from

the company of the blessed, and walk down into the dismal regions of despair, to sit with the last, the only unredeemed, the Judas of his race, and be himself more blessed in the pains of hell, than in the glories of heaven? Who, in the midst of the golden harps and the white wings, knowing that one of his kind, one miserable brother in the old-world-time when men were taught to love their neighbor as themselves, was howling unheeded far below in the vaults of the creation, who, I say, would not feel that he must arise, that he had no choice, that, awful as it was, he must gird his loins, and go down into the smoke and the darkness and the fire, travelling the weary and fearful road into the far country to find his brother?—who, I mean, that had the mind of Christ, that had the love of the Father?[20]

Judas was not a man who died by suicide: he was and is a child of God—this is the story that we sing over every human and every victim. The Father stands at the end of the road and waits for every Judas, and upon seeing him, upon seeing her, runs and embraces and kisses and declares, "Child, you have been found."[21]

---

20. MacDonald, "Love Thy Neighbor," in *Unspoken Sermons*, 72.
21. See Luke 15:32.

Appendix II

Lucifer

And [Jesus] said to them, "I was watching the Accuser fall like lightning out of the sky."

LUKE 10:18

THE NAME LUCIFER HAS, through history, become synonymous with the devil or the satan. Indeed, for many, Lucifer is known as the rebellious angel, cast down from heaven by God, a being of pure evil, a liar, and a murderer. The stories of Lucifer's fall, from pulpits and within church groups, are likely told with a confidence of knowledge, an understanding that, even though we are unable to always explain who God is, or explain his ways, we know exactly who Lucifer is, where he came from, and what he is seeking to do—hold that thought.

As Western society becomes increasingly more secularized, the theological stories relating to Lucifer will become less and less familiar, replaced with a belief that Lucifer is nothing more than an entertaining Netflix show. Indeed, in the UK a new mother hit the headlines recently for naming her newborn baby Lucifer, initially unaware of its religious background and history, saying, "I like the name because I like it, I don't think it stands for the devil, in my eyes."[1]

1. Mills, "Mum Who Named Her Son Lucifer," para. 3.

What is even more interesting, however, is how little most of us actually know about the origins of the name "Lucifer," where it actually came from, what it means, and, most importantly, who it is really speaking about.

The verse we began with, from Luke's Gospel, would eventually, in various Christian traditions, become wedded with a verse from Isaiah.

> How you are fallen from heaven,
> O Day Star, son of Dawn!
> How you are cut down to the ground,
> you who laid the nations low![2]

Isaiah is speaking of the fallen King Nebuchadnezzar II of Babylon. His name is Hêlēl ben Shahar, meaning "Lucifer Son of the Morning." Christian thought, in the early centuries, combined Satan and Lucifer, making the names synonymous with the other, and out of it produced the idea of a fall of an angel called Lucifer before creation. This idea of a pre-cosmic fall of a supreme archangel named "Lucifer" or "Satan" has dominated Christian thought on the origins of evil, yet there is little biblical evidence to support such a reading.

The only angelic rebellion that is hinted at anywhere in Scripture relates to the "sons of Elohim," or angels, in Gen 6:2, but little is actually known about them. We have stories from different mystical traditions that tell us how, because of "the daughters of men," these angelic creatures, out of lust and desire, wanted to wed human women. A few verses later and even stranger creatures appear, known as "nefilim." According to these early texts, the mysterious "nefilim" of Gen 6:6—said to be a new breed of incredible giants—were the offspring of these human-divine relations, the result of sexual relationships between women and the "sons of Elohim." The mystical book of Enoch details two hundred of these sons of Elohim, or "Watchers,"[3] who abandoned heaven, and

---

2. Luke 14:12 (NRSV).

3. The 2014 film *Noah*, directed by Darren Aronofsky, draws heavily from the book of Enoch, and other Jewish mystical sources. The Watchers feature—fallen angels turned into stone giants—as do the first humans clothed in light, until sin enters the garden of Eden. When Noah tells the story of God calling

rebelled, causing chaos. Coming to earth, under the leadership of a Watcher called Semyâzâ, a new home was made. Not only did they become fathers of the nefilim but taught their human wives sorcery, various kinds of magic, enchantments, and also how to use plants and trees, perhaps to make medicine. Azâzêl, one of the other leaders, taught humanity how to make weapons, jewelry, and dye for the skin and hair.

These "children" of the sons of Elohim were monstrous, not only in size but also practice; the nefilim fought and killed each other, as well as killing humans, eating their flesh, and drinking their blood.

According to the book of Enoch, on being informed of the depth of depravity the nefilim have lowered themselves to, God sent the archangel Michael to imprison these monsters in the darkness below, and then slay them; but the ghosts or spirits of the nefilim became demons that roamed the world, bringing destruction and affliction. However, God ordered these spirits and ghosts to be bound in prison, locking them up forever.

The reference, in the New Testament, to Christ journeying to these spirits in order to preach to them[4] seems to echo the account of Enoch journeying to the dwelling of these spirits in order to proclaim God's condemnation upon them.[5]

All of the above serves to explain that the mythology of fallen angels has existed within various strands of Judaic and Christian thought, yet there is little to suggest that, within scriptural tradition, such a reading can be applied to the figure of Lucifer.[6] So what about Luke 10:18?

---

life into existence, it is one of the best visual narratives of the Biblical account of creation ever created.

4. "For the Anointed also suffered, once and for all, a just man on behalf of the unjust, so that he might lead you to God, being put to death in flesh and yet being made alive in spirit, Whereby he also journeyed and made a proclamation to the spirits in prison, To those in the past who disobeyed while God's magnanimity bided its time, in the days of Noah when the ark was being fashioned, by which a few—that is, eight souls—were brought safe through the water." 1 Pet 3:18–20.

5. See 1 Enoch 12–15.

6. For more on this, see Hart, *New Testament*, 392.

> And [Jesus] said to them, "I was watching the Accuser fall like lightning out of the sky."

Quite simply, Jesus, using metaphor and symbolic imagery (something he regularly deployed in his teachings) is highlighting to his disciples that their mission has been remarkable in its success. In other words, in effect Jesus is saying, "The kingdom of God is at hand, and I see the satan removed from power; this cosmic reign is coming to an end." New Testament images of "the Archon of the Power of the air, of the spirit now operating in the sons of disobedience"[7] and the "Archon of this cosmos,"[8] being cast out, follow these ideas of a power here on earth, operating through history, at work within humanity, now falling from its place of power. Such an idea shouldn't surprise us: history is replete with rulers and earthly empires rising and falling in power.

So, then, who is Lucifer? In 2 Pet 1:19, the early Christians are encouraged to wait for the dawn of a new day when "*Phosphoros* will arise in your hearts." *Phosphoros* means "the Light-Bringer," which is translated *Hêlêl* in Hebrew, and *Lucifer* in Latin. It is also the name for Morning Star, which is Venus as seen before dawn. In the final verses of Revelation Jesus declares himself to be "the bright Morning Star."[9] So, while certain Church teachers combined Isa 14:12, "Lucifer Son of the Morning," and Luke 10:18, "Accuser fall like lightning," creating a Satan/Lucifer angelic fall from heaven, the New Testament actually draws a different conclusion: every mention of the Morning Star is one of remarkable hope—the Morning Star appears when the night is at its darkest, meaning the dawn[10] is on its way—and the only person ever identified with this star "Lucifer" is Jesus Christ himself.

---

7. Eph 2:2.
8. John 12:31.
9. Rev 22:16.
10. "But for you who revere my name the sun of righteousness shall rise, with healing in its wings." Mic 4:2 (NRSV). "Through our God's inmost mercy, whereby a dawning from on high will visit us, To shine upon those sitting in darkness and death's shadow, so to guide our feet into the path of peace." Luke 1:78–79.

Appendix III

Death of the Firstborn

Whoever has seen me has seen the Father.
JOHN 14:9

TO UNDERSTAND THE EVENTS of the Exodus narrative we need to first return to the creation narratives of the Torah (the first five books of the Hebrew Scriptures).

> When God began to create the heavens and the earth, the earth was complete chaos, and darkness covered the face of the deep, while a wind from God swept over the face of the waters. Then God said, "Let there be light," and there was light. And God saw that the light was good, and God separated the light from the darkness. God called the light Day, and the darkness he called Night. And there was evening and there was morning, the first day. (Gen 1:1–5 NRSV)

I would argue that the early books of the Hebrew Scriptures are not historical accounts, but theological works, weaving together wisdom and words that reflected the evolving ideas of who God was being discovered to be. This creation myth is telling us something about who God is.

Death of the Firstborn

Ancient cultures from around the world have their own creation myths, very often imagining a world born out of blood and chaos. In some versions of Greek mythology, for instance, Zeus destroys the titans for eating Dionysus, and out of their ashes, humanity is birthed. And then there is the Mesopotamian creation myth, Enuma Elish, which describes Marduk, the chief god, killing the goddess Tiamat, cutting her body in two, and using one half to create the earth. Still other myths from other cultures have the world created from slain giants, decapitated heads, and the blood of great serpents; time and again the earth and humanity emerge from blood and violence. But in these opening verses from Genesis, God creates through breath and Word, nonviolently. The movement is from darkness to light, from chaos to order: "There was evening and there was morning," a phrase repeated throughout these creation verses.

This movement is a theological statement, an expression of who God is, one who leads creation, nonviolently, from chaos into order, from ignorance into understanding, from darkness to light. The plagues of Egypt, then, can be seen from this perspective, of a God who is *being discovered*. As we saw earlier, the *Targum Neofiti*, recognizing the world play between Gen 1 and Exod 3, interprets Exod 3:14 as, "The one who said and the world came into existence from the beginning; and is to say to it again: Be, and it will be, has sent me to you." God is the one who speaks, who says, "Be, and it will be," and thus acts and *brings into being from abundance*, rather than destroying or restricting, a generous God, not a withholding god. This is not a warrior god like Marduk, but one who speaks and listens in response to suffering.

> After a long time the king of Egypt died. The Israelites groaned under their slavery and cried out. Their cry for help rose up to God from their slavery. God heard their groaning, and God remembered his covenant with Abraham, Isaac, and Jacob. God looked upon the Israelites, and God took notice of them. (Exod 2:23–25 NRSV)

The Hebrew word used for cry, here, is *sa'aq*, an expression of pain or being wounded, a cry for help, and a question asking if anybody

Appendix III

saw: "Will anyone come to my help?" Walter Brueggemann says that the Exodus cry is the "primal scream that permits the beginning of history." Brueggemann argues that *sa'aq* is "a cry of misery and wretchedness," and is, as such, "a militant sense of being wronged with the powerful expectation that it will be heard and answered."[1]

The Israelites, then, have been heard, which is a remarkable shift in ancient understandings of God: one who actually hears an oppressed people in their suffering. But that does not mean God violently responds to this oppression. Rather, God walks alongside them in their pain, symbolized by fire in the burning bush to Moses,[2] a pillar of cloud in the desert by day as the Israelites escaped Egypt, and a pillar of fire by night. Remember, since the dawn of creation God is seeking to build a table of reconciliation, where enemies come together and are united in peace (Ps 23), a table that God will be present at. What, then, of the death of the Egyptian firstborn?

Throughout *Finding God*, we have been discovering the myth stories created to justify scapegoating and conceal murder. The blood of Abel calls out from the ground for vengeance, and it would be easy to concede that the plagues upon Egypt were acts of vengeance from God in response to the suffering of the Israelites. As such, when interpreted through a lens of blood vengeance and sacred violence, these natural events could be seen as God's righteous judgment against oppressors. But God has no enemies. The blood of Jesus speaks peace—a better word than vengeance desired by the blood of Abel.

We seek scapegoats in a time of chaos and crisis as the community collapses. According to the story within the text, the heart of the Egyptian kingdom is being torn apart by natural disasters, *perceived* to be divine judgments. The Egyptians blame the Israelites, eventually desiring their expulsion, and the Israelites claim

---

1. Brueggemann, *Prophetic Imagination*, 11–12.

2. In certain streams of Orthodox thought, the burning bush represents the universe, the fire of God's glory infusing, filling, and burning across its entire existence, yet never consuming or destroying it.

God's justice at the death of the Egyptians. There would be no reason for people living within a time "constructed on generative violence"[3] to believe any differently; God/gods deliver supreme will and favor through violence, and that violence maintains the cohesion and preservation of a group. But as readers of the text, and as those reading the text through the lens of a God who is nonviolent in character and nature, the death of the firstborn can be interpreted differently.

In his book, *Seven Stories*, Anthony Bartlett argues that each plague can be understood as natural calamities that have fallen upon the Egyptian kingdom, the final plague a natural consequence of all that has gone before.[4] Because of the poor weather and plague of locusts (something that still occurs in the Middle East), the meagre harvest of grain has been stored damp, in silos, creating a breeding ground for mycotoxins: "The eldest child would receive double rations leading to increased death rates among the first born."[5]

There is more to the text, however, which brings us back to theology: God is continually seeking to move humanity from the darkness of sin to the light of freedom, found in divine relationship. Gregory of Nyssa calls for a spiritual reading of the text, and believes the death of the firstborn is a spiritual insight that is also taught in the gospel: kill the beginning of sin within your life, "lust before adultery . . . anger before murder."[6] Whatever the history might be, what matters most are the spiritual truths, how this text is leading us, by the Spirit, into deeper communion with God. The Nyssan continues,

---

3. Bartlett, *Seven Stories*, 58.

4. The death of the livestock could be because of disease caused by excessive flies; the swarm of flies a result of mass animal death, including dead frogs, who had escaped contaminated water, but then died; contaminated water would kill the fish (producing more flies), the "blood" color of the river a result of certain microorganisms that make the water red and toxic. For more on this see Raver, "Biblical Plagues."

5. Bartlett, *Seven Stories*, 59.

6. Gregory of Nyssa, *Life of Moses*, 42.

APPENDIX III

> Therefore, as we look for the true spiritual meaning, seeking to determine whether the events took place typologically, we should be prepared to believe that the lawgiver has taught through the things said. The teaching is this: When through virtue one comes to grips with any evil, he must completely destroy the first beginnings of evil.[7]

We continue to live in a world ravished by natural disasters, plagues, disease, and calamity. It is a world groaning and in pain, waiting for rebirth into glory (Rom 8:18–22). A story like the plagues, then, should not surprise us, such is the nature of a "sin-sick" world we live in.[8] What surprises us—and should now liberate us—as we have discovered throughout this book, is a God who does not cause such suffering.

As our perception of God changes, we see how, in the birth, life, teachings, death, and resurrection of Jesus, God declares "peace" over all things—and has always declared peace. From here the Exodus story shifts within us.

---

7. Gregory of Nyssa, *Life of Moses*, 42–43.
8. See Hauerwas, "Sinsick," 7–21.

Appendix IV

Holiness

And I, when I am lifted up from the earth, will drag everyone to me.
John 12:32

There was a belief, seen in various ways throughout the biblical writings, that the community of faith was like a fortress, a place of refuge where the will and purposes of God would be fulfilled. Take the psalmist, for instance:

> For God alone my soul waits in silence,
> for my hope is from him.
> He alone is my rock and my salvation,
> my fortress; I shall not be shaken.
> On God rests my deliverance and my honor;
> my mighty rock, my refuge is in God.
> trust in him at all times, O people;
> pour out your heart before him;
> God is a refuge for us. (Ps 62:5–8 NRSV)

The psalmist is using symbolic language of the eschatological hope in who God is; a place of refuge. This language of eschatological refuge found in God is developed within the teachings of Christ, often in parabolic form, such as the sheep being carried to safety, or the lost son being welcomed home, and the promise of true rest,

Appendix IV

something that can only happen when we are no longer in danger. What does it mean, then, to be safe?

Jesus gathers and calls to himself all people—including those regarded as outcasts—so that they might find refuge in him. What does this have to do with holiness? I would suggest that holiness is primarily about *who we are gathered to*, rather than what we are separated from. To be holy (set apart) is to be gathered *into* the life of God where sin has no place. Within certain Christian theological traditions, holiness is about expunging sin from the community, and sending it away in order to "cleanse" the community from the sin infecting it. Holiness, then, has primarily been understood as *casting out* rather than *gathering in*, being "other" rather than "together." So then, what about when we speak of God's holiness? What can we say?

To say God is holy does not mean God is set apart. Why do I say that? Well, think of when there was only God: God, Ultimate Being, in eternal perichoresis,[1] a dance of love between Father, Son, and Spirit. In this "moment" there was God and nothing else. When we try and think of "nothing" we always think of "something," whether it's space, or darkness, or an abyss, it is always *something* we are thinking of; thinking of nothing is impossible. But before anything existed, there was only God. Therefore, there was nothing for God to be set apart from. God's holiness, therefore, is not determined by creation; God has always been holy. So we must consider God's holiness in other ways.

Notice in the Gospel accounts how Jesus *goes to* people—the outcasts, sinners, lepers—in order to reveal God to them, and show them the true nature of who God is. Certainly, Jesus also

---

1. "For they are without interval between them and inseparable and their mutual indwelling [*en allais perichoresin*] is without confusion." Kimel, "St. John of Damascus," quoting *An Exposition of the Orthodox Faith* (brackets in original). *Perichoresis* is a word used by various church writers through the centuries to describe the eternal indwelling relationship of God. We could think of it as a relationship of divine dance, each Person of the Trinitarian life freely responding in love to the other, each giving way to the other in unconditionality. It is a dance of creativity and freedom, one all things are invited to share in.

withdraws, but that is always in resistance to the will of the crowd, refusing the mimetic rivalry and desire that always consumes a group of people. Jesus enters the space people inhabit and infuses them with his life, and character, and holiness; his life becomes our life. Whereas holiness was seen as avoidance, Jesus goes to people and heals them, blesses them, loves them, and imparts grace to them; they receive from him. Holiness is what God gives, to share in divine life. As multiple church fathers said in one way or another, "God becomes human so that we might become god." We could say that holiness is being set apart from slavery to death by being joined to Christ. Whatever God touches becomes holy, and the life, death, and resurrection of Jesus reveals a God who touches the whole of creation, and brings it into the life of relationship.

God's holiness, then, is about how God, through effervescent love, enables all things to become what they are destined and created for, found in complete communion with the Trinitarian life. Our holiness is not about being separated from but being joined to, called out of the darkness of death into the light of God's life.

Bibliography

Alighieri, Dante. *Dante's Inferno*. Translated by Henry Francis Cary. New York: Pollard and Moss, 1885.
Antonello, Pierpaolo, and Paul Gifford, eds. *How We Became Human: Mimetic Theory and the Science of Evolutionary Origins*. Studies in Violence, Mimesis, and Culture. East Lansing: Michigan State University Press, 2015.
Augustine. *Patrologia Latina*. Vol. 38. Paris: Migne, 1841.
Bailey, Kenneth E. *Jesus Through Middle Eastern Eyes: Cultural Studies in the Gospels*. Downers Grove, IL: InterVarsity, 2008.
Bailie, Gil. *Violence Unveiled: Humanity at the Crossroads*. New York: Crossroad, 1999.
Barth, Karl. *Church Dogmatics*. Vols. 1–4. Translated and edited by G. W. Bromiley and T. F. Torrance. Edinburgh: T&T Clark, 1956–75.
Bartlett, Anthony W. *Seven Stories: How to Teach the Nonviolent Bible*. New York: Hopetime, 2017.
Blatty, William Peter. *The Exorcist*. London: Penguin Random House, 2024.
Bonhoeffer, Dietrich. *Ethics*. Minneapolis: Fortress, 2000.
———. *Letters and Papers from Prison*. London: SCM, 1967.
Brueggemann, Walter. *The Prophetic Imagination*. Minneapolis: Fortress, 2001.
Calvin, John. *Institutes of the Christian Religion*. Edited by J. T. McNeill. Translated by F. L. Battles. Philadelphia: Westminster, 1960.
Charles, R. H., ed. "Book of Enoch." In *The Apocrypha and Pseudepigrapha of the Old Testament in English*. Oxford: Clarendon, 1913. Revised by Joshua Williams. Christian Classics Ethereal Library, 1995. https://www.ccel.org/c/charles/otpseudepig/enoch/enoch_2.htm.
Clement. *The First Epistle of Clement*. In *Ante-Nicene Fathers of the Christian Church*, vol. 1, edited by James Donaldson et al., 5–21. Edinburgh: T&T Clark, 1866–95.
Colwell, John E. *Promise and Presence: An Exploration of Sacramental Theology*. Carlisle, UK: Paternoster, 2005.
———. *The Rhythm of Doctrine: A Liturgical Sketch of Christian Faith and Faithfulness*. Milton Keynes: Paternoster, 2007.
Cone, James H. *Black Theology and Black Power*. New York: Orbis, 1997.

BIBLIOGRAPHY

———. *A Black Theology of Liberation*. New York: Orbis, 2010.

———. *The Cross and the Lynching Tree*. New York: Orbis, 2011.

Dave [David Orobosa Omoregie]. "Black." Warner Chappell Music, Kobalt Music, 2019.

Dawkins, Richard. *The God Delusion*. London: Transworld, 2007.

Death Penalty Information Center. "Murder Rate of Death Penalty States Compared to Non-Death Penalty States." Death Penalty Information Center. https://deathpenaltyinfo.org/facts-and-research/murder-rates/murder-rate-of-death-penalty-states-compared-to-non-death-penalty-states.

Earl, Douglas Scotohu. "Reading Joshua as Christian Scripture." PhD thesis, University of Durham, 2008. Durham e-Theses. http://etheses.dur.ac.uk/2267.

Edwards, Jonathan. "Sinners in the Hands of an Angry God." Blue Letter Bible. https://www.blueletterbible.org/Comm/edwards_jonathan/Sermons/Sinners.cfm.

Epistle to Diognetus, The. In *Ante-Nicene Fathers of the Christian Church*, vol. 1, edited by James Donaldson et al., 25–30. Edinburgh: T&T Clark, 1866–95.

Eusebius. *Church History*. In *Nicene and Post-Nicene Fathers, Second Series*, vol. 1, translated by Arthur Cushman McGiffert, edited by Philip Schaff and Henry Wace. Buffalo, NY: Christian Literature, 1890. Revised and edited by Kevin Knight. New Advent. https://www.newadvent.org/fathers/250110.htm.

Finley, M. I. *Ancient Economy*. London: University of California Press, 1999.

Flanagan, Mike, dir. *The Fall of the House of Usher*. Season 1, episode 2, "The Masque of the Red Death." Aired Oct. 12, 2023, on Netflix.

———, dir. *The Haunting of Hill House*. Season 1, episode 1, "Steven Sees a Ghost." Aired Oct. 12, 2018, on Netflix.

Gifford, Paul. "Homo Religiosus in Mimetic Perspective: An Evolutionary Dialogue." In *How We Became Human: Mimetic Theory and the Science of Evolutionary Origins*, edited by Pierpaolo Antonello and Paul Gifford, 307–38. Studies in Violence, Mimesis, and Culture. East Lansing: Michigan State University Press, 2015.

Girard, René. "Generative Scapegoating." In *Violent Origins: Walter Burket, René Girard, and Jonathan Z. Smith on Ritual Killing and Cultural Formation*, edited by Robert G. Hamerton-Kelly, 73–147. Stanford, CA: Stanford University Press, 1987.

———. *I See Satan Fall like Lightning*. New York: Orbis, 1999.

———. *Things Hidden Since the Foundation of the World*. London: Continuum, 2003.

———. *Violence and the Sacred*. Baltimore: John Hopkins University Press, 1977.

Gregory of Nyssa. *Homilies on the Beatitudes*. Edited by Hubertus Drobner et al. Leiden: Brill, 2000.

———. *The Life of Moses*. Translated by Abraham J. Malherbe and Everett Ferguson. San Francisco: HarperSanFrancisco, 2008.

———. *On the Soul and Resurrection*. Translated by Catherine P. Roth. New York: St. Vladimir's Seminary, 1993.
Gunton, Colin. *A Brief Theology of Revelation*. Edinburgh: T&T Clark, 1995.
Häkkinen, Sakari. "Poverty in the First-Century Galilee." *HTS Theological Studies* 72:4 (2016) a3398. https://doi.org/10.4102/hts.v72i4.3398.
Hardin, Michael. *The Jesus Driven Life*. Lancaster, PA: JDL, 2010.
———. *Mimetic Theory and Biblical Interpretation: Reclaiming the Good News of the Gospel*. Eugene, OR: Cascade, 2017.
———. "The Satan." *Clarion Journal for Religion, Peace, and Justice*, July 15, 2021. https://www.clarion-journal.com/clarion_journal_of_spirit/2021/07/the-satan-michael-hardin.html.
Harris, Thomas. *The Hannibal Lecter Trilogy*. London: Heinemann, 2005.
Hart, David Bentley. *Atheist Delusions*. London: Yale University Press, 2009.
———. *The Experience of God: Being, Consciousness, Bliss*. London: Yale University Press, 2013.
———. *The New Testament: A Translation*. London: Yale University Press, 2017.
———. *The Story of Christianity*. London: Quercus, 2009.
———. *Tradition and Apocalypse: An Essay in the Future of Christian Belief*. Grand Rapids: Baker Academic, 2022.
Hauerwas, Stanley. *Matthew*. Grand Rapids: Brazos, 2006.
———. "Sinsick." In *Sin, Death, and the Devil*, edited by Carl E. Braaten and Robert W. Jenson, 7–21. Grand Rapids: Eerdmans, 2000.
Haward, Joseph. *Be Afraid: How Horror and Faith Can Change the World*. Eugene, OR: Wipf and Stock, 2018.
———. *Every Last Drop*. Chicago: Anxiety, 2024.
———. *The Ghost of Perfection: Searching for Humanity*. Eugene, OR: Resource, 2017.
———. "Twin Speaks." In *Suicide: An Anthology*, edited by Jon Lindsey et al., 186–97. Las Vegas: House of Vlad, 2024.
Hesiod. *Theogony*. Theoi. https://www.theoi.com/Text/HesiodTheogony.html.
Hitchens, Christopher. *God Is Not Great: How Religion Poisons Everything*. London: Atlantic, 2008.
Hitler, Adolf. *Mein Kampf*. Mumbai: Jaico, 2007.
Irenaeus. *Against Heresies*. In *Ante-Nicene Fathers of the Christian Church*, vol. 1, edited by James Donaldson et al., 315–567. Edinburgh: T&T Clark, 1866–95.
Isaac of Nineveh. *The Second Part, Chapters IV–XLI*. Translated by Sebastian Brock. Walpole, MA: Peeters, 1995.
Justin Martyr. *First Apology*. In *Ante-Nicene Fathers of the Christian Church*, vol. 1, edited by James Donaldson et al., 159–302. Edinburgh: T&T Clark, 1866–95.
Kaminsky, Joel S. "Joshua 7: A Reassessment of Israelite Conceptions of Corporate Punishment." In *The Pitcher Is Broken: Memorial Essays for Gösta W. Ahlström*, edited by Steven W. Holloway and Lowell K. Handy, 315–46. Sheffield: Sheffield Academic, 1995.

Bibliography

Kierkegaard, Søren. *Fear and Trembling*. Translated by Alistair Hannay. Reading, UK: Penguin, 2005.

Kimel, Aidan. "St. John of Damascus on the Holy Trinity." *Eclectic Orthodoxy* (blog), May 3, 2016. https://afkimel.wordpress.com/2016/05/03/st-john-of-damascus-on-the-holy-trinity.

King, Martin Luther, Jr. "Nonviolence and Racial Justice." In *The Papers of Martin Luther King, Jr.*, vol. 4, *Symbol of the Movement, January 1957–December 1958*, edited by Clayborne Carson, 118–22. London: University of California Press, 2000.

———. *Strength to Love*. Glasgow: Fount, 1981.

———. *Where Do We Go From Here? Chaos or Community?* Boston: Beacon, 2010.

Lurie, Alan. "Is Religion the Cause of Most Wars?" *HuffPost* (blog), June 10, 2012. https://www.huffpost.com/entry/is-religion-the-cause-of_b_1400766.

Luther, Martin. "Heidelberg Disputation." Book of Concord. https://thebookofconcord.org/sources-and-context/heidelberg-disputation.

MacDonald, George. *Unspoken Sermons, Series I*. London: Strahan, 1867. Reprint, Grand Rapids: Christian Classics Ethereal Library. Page references are to electronic reprint. https://www.ccel.org/ccel/m/macdonald/unspoken1/cache/unspoken1.pdf.

McNamara, Martin, trans. *The Aramaic Bible: Targum Neofiti 1*. Collegeville, MN: Liturgical, 1994.

Mills, Kelly-Ann. "Mum Who Named Her Son Lucifer Says She Has Been Slammed by Online Trolls." *Mirror*, Jan. 11, 2022. https://www.mirror.co.uk/news/uk-news/mum-who-named-son-lucifer-25912100.

Navarro, Guillermo, dir. *Hannibal*. Season 1, episode 5, "Coquilles." Written by Scott Nimerfro and Bryan Fuller. Aired Apr. 25, 2013, on NBC.

Nolan, Christopher, dir. *The Prestige*. Burbank, CA: Warner Bros., 2006.

Oka, Rahul C., et al. "Population Is the Main Driver of War Group Size and Conflict Casualties." *Proceedings of the National Academy of Sciences* 114:52 (2017) E11101–E11110. https://doi.org/10.1073/pnas.1713972114.

Origen. *Against Celsus*. In *Ante-Nicene Fathers of the Christian Church*, vol. 4, edited by James Donaldson et al., 675–1187. Edinburgh: T&T Clark, 1866–95.

———. *Homilies on Joshua*. Translated by Barbara J. Bruce. Edited by Cynthia White. Washington, DC: Catholic University of America Press, 2002.

———. *The Song of Songs: Commentary and Homilies*. Translated by R. P. Lawson. New York: Newman, 1957.

Papavassiliou, Vassilios. *The Ancient Faith Prayer Book*. Chesterton, IN: Ancient Faith, 2014.

Paynter, Helen. "Towards a Biblical Theology of Herem." Master's diss., Bristol Baptist College, 2011. https://www.academia.edu/12813335/Towards_a_Biblical_Theology_of_Herem.

Pelikan, Jaraslov. *Christianity and Classical Culture*. London: Yale University Press, 1993.

Bibliography

Philostratus, Flavius. *The Life of Apollonius of Tyana, the Epistles of Apollonius and the Treatise by Eusebius*. Vol. 1. Loeb Classical Library. Translated by F. C. Conybeare. Cambridge, MA: Harvard University Press, 1948.

Ramsay, Julius, dir. *The Walking Dead*. Season 5, episode 10, "Them." Aired Feb. 15, 2015, on AMC.

Raver, Anne. "Biblical Plagues: A Novel Theory." *New York Times*, Apr. 4, 1996. https://www.nytimes.com/1996/04/04/garden/biblical-plagues-a-novel-theory.html.

Schwager, Raymond. *Must There Be Scapegoats? Violence and Redemption in the Bible*. New York: Crossroad, 1987.

Scott, Ridley, dir. *Blade Runner*. Burbank, CA: Warner Bros. Pictures, 1982.

Tertullian. *De Spectaculis*. In *Ante-Nicene Fathers of the Christian Church*, vol. 3, edited by James Donaldson et al., 79–91. Edinburgh: T&T Clark, 1866–95.

Wachowskis, The, dirs. *The Matrix*. Written by the Wachowskis. Burbank, CA: Warner Bros., 1999.

Weaver, Denny J. *The Nonviolent Atonement*. Grand Rapids: Eerdmans, 2001.

Wells, Samuel. *God's Companions: Christian Ethics and the Abundance of God*. Oxford: Blackwell, 2006.

Wink, Walter. *Engaging the Powers*. Minneapolis: Fortress, 1992.

Žižek, Slavoj. *Enjoy Your Symptom! Jacques Lacan in Hollywood and Out*. New York: Routledge, 2008.

———. *God in Pain: Inversions of Apocalypse*. New York: Seven Stories, 2012.

———. *Living in the End Times*. London, Verso, 2010.

www.ingramcontent.com/pod-product-compliance
Lightning Source LLC
Chambersburg PA
CBHW070459090426
42735CB00012B/2621